In loving memory of my mother,
Karen Royer.

As an extra way to share her love . . .

We wanted to honor my mother in this book and we knew a fun way to do that would be to kick it off with sharing her very favorite pie. It takes a base pie filling and "fixes it up" the good old fashion mom way! It is a simple one to make and it is delicious!

———— JB & Jamie ————

DR KAREN'S PUMPKIN PIE

Prep Time: 10 min   Cook Time: 45-55 min   Yields: 8 servings

Preheat oven to 350°F.

Combine pie filling, sugar, seasonings, milk, and eggs in a bowl and mix well.

Pour into pie crust.

Bake for 45-55 minutes or until your knife comes out clean.

1 16-oz can Libby's Pumpkin Pie Filling

3/4 cup sugar

1/2 tsp salt

2 tbsp ground cinnamon

1/2 tsp ground ginger

1/4 tsp ground cloves

6 oz evaporated milk

2 eggs, beaten

1 10" Royers Pie Crust (p. 243)

Cooking With JB & Jamie
Royers Round Top Cafe

Copyright © 2022 by Jonathan (JB) and Jamie Royer

Published by Lucid Books in Houston, TX
www.LucidBooks.com

Photography by Megan Poling

eISBN: 978-1-63296-504-2 (eBook)
ISBN: 978-1-63296-505-9 (paperback)
ISBN: 978-1-63296-506-6 (hardback)

ROYERS ROUND TOP CAFE

COOKING
WITH JB
& Jamie

LUCIDBOOKS

Hey y'all!

Thank you for inviting us into your home. We're going to talk to you like family because at Royers Cafe, you enter as a guest and leave as family—full of good food and great memories.

Cooking is a lost art, and too many people aren't eating together around the table anymore. Over the years, we have been blessed to watch food bring many people together, and we felt we needed to do something about it. We knew that if we could share some of our recipes— simple recipes that make great food—we could be part of helping you gather your loved ones at the table to connect and build cherished memories. As crazy as our world can get and as divisive as views can be, coming together for a conversation over good food can be a unifying experience.

It has always been our mission to show others that great food can be cooked in their very own kitchen— that's why we started our live, local events. Our Cooking Classes, Wine Dinners, Date Nights, Community Catering, and Holiday Gatherings are all special to us, but we also wanted to share our recipes with those who aren't right here at our doorstep.

Food doesn't have to be complicated to be good. That's why the recipes in this cookbook are simple but packed with flavor. We don't do half the stuff that fancy French chefs do, but we do put out a good meal, and we want to teach you how to do that as well. We'll show you how easy it is to make pie dough, cook a filet, whip up a savory sauce, and not screw up a good cut of meat.

You can take any recipe in this book and say, "I can make this," and you can find every ingredient in your local grocery store. Read the instructions, plan ahead, and gather your ingredients. It really is as easy as that. The recipes are simple but elevated—what Bud Royer used to call "sophisticated comfort food." And when you put a little bit of love into it, you'll have a heck of a meal.

Every recipe in this book is our actual recipe, and every photograph is food we really cooked. In most food photography, the food you see is not actually the food you would eat. *(The milk in cereal bowls is not milk. Did you know that it is typically white glue? The soups have wax added to them. They use shoe polish to make grill marks! Most of the food photographed isn't even fully cooked in those shots.)* But we didn't go down that road. Yes, we want beautiful images that will make your mouth water, but more importantly, we want you to know what the recipe will actually look like coming out of your kitchen. So we simply took a true shot of the food immediately after we plated it.

We've put a lot of love and hard work into these recipes. They're fun and easy to make, and you'll want to share them. That's the whole point—gathering together in your kitchen can lead to hours around your table and memories that last a lifetime.

Along with the recipes, you'll find tips for cooking, planning meals, and using a variety of tools in your kitchen. You don't need a lot of fancy gadgets to make good food, but a handful of the right tools will get you started on the right foot.

Enjoy this small window into our story, our life, our restaurant, and our passion for real food, real ingredients, real flavor, and real cooking!

———————— JB & Jamie ————————

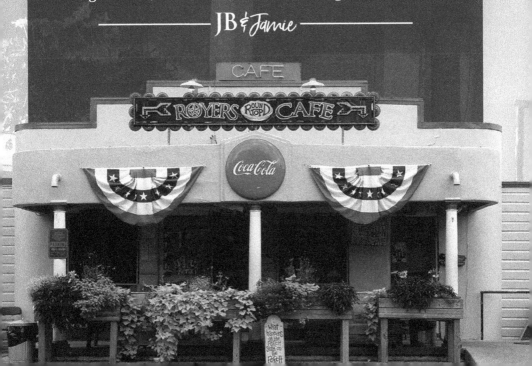

TABLE OF CONTENTS

AROUND THE TABLE
Anita & Rick Perry

Every time Anita and I pass through the screen door to Royers Round Top Cafe, I feel like a slice of heaven has been served à la mode. This treasure of a country eatery just down the road from our home draws folks making the road trip from Houston to Austin, or vice versa, five days a week. Like us, they come for the sights, sounds, and smells of a country cafe that dishes up big-city-level goodness. The steak melts in your mouth, the cheese grits come with an extra kick of jalapeño, and the apple pie will take you back in time to your mom's kitchen. Royers has it all—"stuff that grazes," "stuff that oinks and chirps," and "stuff that swims."

Now you don't have to pile the family into the car and drive to Round Top because you can turn your own kitchen into a Royers satellite cafe with this special edition of the *Cooking with JB and Jamie* cookbook.

Known for its antiquing, its historic churches and buildings that were rescued and rehabbed, and a theater as ornate as any in Europe, the town of Round Top, Texas, population 90, is a well-known Texas treasure. And Royers Round Top Cafe is there. It has earned a far-reaching reputation for quality food—especially its pies.

Bud "the PieMan" Royer and his late wife, Dr. Karen, opened Royers doors in 1987 after they took over a tiny cafe. Over the years, it has truly been a family business, with Bud, Karen, and their four children turning this small-town cafe into their labor of love. Today, JB and his wife, Jamie-Len, are turning out good food within sight of Round Top's one stoplight.

Royers is not only a welcome sight for locals and globetrotters alike, but it also ships mail order pies to customers in every state in the country. Their word-of-mouth marketing effort, sustained by mouthwatering meals, has made Royers a Texas institution with national appeal.

We will make you a promise: make just one meal out of this cookbook, and it will replace Betty Crocker on your dining room table!

Enjoy!
Anita & Rick Perry

AROUND THE TABLE
Kassie Alexander

Years ago, my husband, Corey, met JB in our local gym, and they quickly hit it off. Shortly after they met, the Cafe posted about their upcoming Valentine's Day reservations. That Valentine's Day dinner proved to be the first of many celebrations at the Cafe, from special occasions and holidays to simple family dinners or date nights.

JB made us feel right at home that first dinner, serving us amazing food and wine with that big grin of his—and then to top it off, he generously covered our tab. We were shocked and wanted to return the favor, but we didn't know how to pull it off. I mean, what do you cook for *the Royers*? So I did what any girl would do in my position . . . I called my mama! Help! My mom was raised in New Orleans, so we settled on fixing a family favorite: Crawfish Pie. Thankfully, we made fast friends with JB and his wife, Jamie, that night over the crawfish pie, drinking gin and tonics by the pool while our kids swam. All that stress for nothing!

We've become the best of friends and have since spent countless meals, vacations, and holidays together.

What I've learned through the years from JB and Jamie is that delicious recipes don't have to be difficult. The most important part of any meal is the people who are gathering around the table. Don't get me wrong, I've made a lot of the recipes in this cookbook and eaten most of them too! Good food like this makes for an even more enjoyable evening. Have fun cooking for those joining your table. Just don't forget to keep the main thing the main thing!

Kassie Alexander

AROUND THE TABLE
Diane Keller

My relationship with JB and Jamie grew out of the friendship my daughter and son-in-law, Kassie and Corey Alexander, started years ago around the time Kassie cried for help, "What do I cook for the Royers when they come for dinner?" My husband and I shared a mutual love for cooking with JB and Jamie, and the Crawfish Pie we made led us to many "Cooking with JB Classes," wine pairing dinners, and a multitude of meals at the Cafe. At the Cafe or at home, Jamie and JB always establish a warm and welcoming atmosphere, and the delicious food is the added bonus with these friends we now consider family!

Because of my love for cooking and gathering with friends and family around the table, I am a collector of cookbooks from everywhere I travel and from chefs I enjoy. Something I always consider when purchasing a new cookbook is whether the recipes call for ingredients I can easily find and instructions that are simple to follow. That is one reason I have enjoyed the Cooking with JB Classes— the recipes they share are always delightful and made with ingredients I can find in small-town Brenham. You won't be disappointed with any recipe in this cookbook, and they will help you create your own welcoming atmosphere for those you bring into your home. Try the recipes. You'll like them!

Diane "Mimi" Keller

OUR STORY
JB & Jamie Royer

Royers Cafe sits in the middle of one of the smallest towns in America. In fact, the 2020 census counted only 90 residents! But today, if you ask people what put Round Top, Texas, on the map, most will tell you it was Royers Cafe. Our family sacrificed a lot to get here and make that happen, and I'm really proud of that.

My dad, Bud "the PieMan", started Royers Cafe in 1987 on a $200 handshake agreement. My parents had to borrow someone's credit card to buy enough gas to get from Houston to Round Top, and my mom put up her grand piano as collateral on a loan.

It wasn't easy being the new family in a small town where everyone knew everyone. Some embraced us, but others were skeptical of the new folks up from Houston—and Bud didn't always make it easy for them. He was a man on a mission, and it takes time in such a small town for the locals to embrace change, let alone change that came with such character. Mom kept us grounded through it all. She ran that kitchen—a Texas kitchen—before it had A/C! Even when she was cooking at the Cafe, she made sure we always gathered around the table for a home-cooked meal. It was around that table that great conversations happened. Our friends often said, "I want to go to your house and have dinner because our family doesn't sit around the table like y'all do." We lived in a five-story silo with a kitchen no bigger than a dining table—about 5' x 10'—on the second floor. It was a very small kitchen, but everything was in there. I'd come home from school at 4:00 p.m., and Mom would have music playing and the table decorated for the season. The place always smelled like a scent from a candle—pumpkin or cinnamon spice. To this day, that scent takes me back.

Mom curated a loving environment, and that was one of the greatest things she did for all of us. It was always a joy to come home to her. She was a saint for knowing exactly what each of us needed. Mom was able to wrangle the kids and continue to support Dad, and neither was an easy job. She's in heaven now, and she deserves her wings and crown—I can tell you that right now. She wasn't just a great mother; she was also a great pillar for Dad. She supported Dad and said, "Hey, run with your dream, and make it happen." She simply went along with the flow, smoothed out his rough edges, and encouraged all of us while making it all look easy. I believe firmly she's the reason each of us has chased our own dreams. There were no guarantees the Cafe would be a success, but she was very supportive, giving, and loving along the way.

My dad was a little difficult to work with at times, but to this day I value his drive to make Royers

Cafe successful. He didn't know how to cook, but he knew what he liked to eat. He understood good service, and he was great at marketing. He saw beyond just running a restaurant—the Cafe was a business. Dad started newsletters, mail-order pies, and bottled sauces. He was one of the first pioneers of shipping food.

He also had an eye for detail and attended to a level of service that very few people could see. He critiqued everyone's work and gave them honest advice. At times, this was hard to hear (and still is!), but as I have grown older, I have also realized why he had many of those "hard" conversations. A lot of times, people don't want to be honest with each other, but Bud wanted the best out of people and the best out of the Cafe. He told the cooks, "Hey, throw this in there," or "Do it this way" because he knew what served his palate well and wanted us to deliver that to our customers. We continue to strive to bring our best to our customers—and I am pretty sure that drive came from Dad.

Our attention to taste is part of the ongoing legacy of the Cafe. My wife, Jamie, and I went to a nice restaurant once and had an incredible meal, but we walked away saying, "I am sure we could match this and maybe even do better." We said, "That quail was good, but I like our quail at the Cafe better." Or we sometimes said, "I loved the lobster BLT, but our shrimp BLT blows it out of the water." That focus on taste started with Dad, and we will continue to keep that legacy strong. Honestly, I am not sure we could stop it if we tried. When we try a new food, I think our brains can't help processing the flavors, and somewhere deep inside, we smile as we think about whether a new flavor or experience has a home in our restaurant.

Bud was part of understanding and maintaining the flavor of the restaurant, but he had many roles. He has always been larger than life in many ways and always opportunistic. He worked hard to get the Cafe recognized regionally and then statewide. In 1988, a year after we started the Cafe, we were voted "Best Country Cafe" in the state of Texas. Later, the *Houston Chronicle* did a story on us, and then *USA Today, CBS Sunday Morning News*, and eventually the Food Network. All that coverage kept making the Cafe and Round Top bigger and bigger.

Of course, you can't talk about Round Top, Texas, without talking about the antique shows. It is magical getting to see people from around the world each fall and spring. It's like going to camp and meeting up with rare friends. Round Top goes from being a weekend escape for people from nearby Houston and Dallas to hosting about 250,000 people for two and a half weeks. We know we're going to be exhausted, but we also know that we get to serve people we see only every six months.

The antique show schedule can be a hard time. We don't see our kids more than eight hours a week - just to wake them up, feed them breakfast, and take them to my parents' house. But it also recharges our batteries to see the patrons who come to every show and the people from California, New York, Florida, or wherever.

Many meet up every antique show at Rogers and relive past memories and create new ones. It's community on steroids as the Cafe helps bring people together to enjoy that camaraderie and experience. It is an energy I can't explain. And it keeps the Cafe on the map.

It sure keeps the Cafe busy, but I'm used to busyness. I was about seven years old when my dad started the Cafe, and by the time I was 12, I was bussing tables and then worked in the kitchen. By 15, I did all the ordering, and at 17, I moved back to the floor, waiting tables and greeting people. I guess I've worked about every job there is in the Cafe!

After growing up in the Cafe, it made sense for me to continue the family business. When I was growing up, I didn't know what I wanted to do. Whenever someone asked, "What do you want to do with your life?" I said, "Be a football coach." I never even played football. But in many ways, running a restaurant, leading Cooking Classes, and hosting Wine Dinners is like coaching a team. You cast a vision like a coach would and communicate what winning looks like each day. I help the crew at the Cafe find a place there and try to bring out the best in people. I love to be around people, encouraging them and building relationships with them. That's where my joy comes in working with food. Our friends come to see us at the Cafe, we get to hang out and encourage one another, and we get to feed them a delicious meal. What's better than that?

Maybe one thing better is working all day with your wife! If he's the head coach, I guess that makes me the assistant coach. I love to make his dreams come alive. He has a lot of them, although some of them make me say, "Listen here: There's no time for that." But it almost always ends in a laugh, and we keep brainstorming. He's the dreamer, and I'm the maker. We work well together like that.

Working side-by-side with JB is fun, and it honestly saved our marriage. I was a trauma tech in the emergency room for 11 years. When we moved to Brenham, Texas, I got a job in the lab here. I was there 10 months, and our schedules were completely opposite. It felt like we were nearing a divorce just because we never saw each other. When I got home, he left for the Café. When we did see each other, we were tired and ended up fighting. On July 4, 2013, after the parade was over and the Café opened, we prayed and talked about it. We decided I would work at the Café. That way, we could be together and focus on our relationship. We still argue at times, but we fight a lot more when we aren't together!

It was an adjustment at first, but now I could not imagine being anywhere else. I absolutely love it. I love the people-most of the time. I'm not much of a talker like JB. He talks a lot, and I'm quiet. But I love cooking, which is crazy because I would never have thought I would. When we got married, I was a picky eater. The only thing I really ate was bean-and-cheese burritos and grilled cheese. I could not cook anything!

After we got married, JB started teaching me. At first, he said, "I know how to cook for a hundred people. I don't know how to cook for two." It took a while for us to figure that out. We had a lot of Hamburger Helper and Jack in the Box until we learned how to cook for two instead of an army. Then while I was on maternity leave with our first daughter, Sadie, I watched a lot of cooking shows and got more interested in cooking.

When I started working at the Café, I mainly did office work like food costs. Slowly I started moving into the kitchen and learning from our cooks: Audrey, Wendy, and Rick. Before I knew it, I was in there full-time and loving it!

Now I love to cook and create new things and lead the other chefs. I think my work as an emergency room tech helped me easily adjust to the planning, prepping, and getting food ready to go. It's definitely satisfying to watch somebody finish a meal and hear them say, "Best steak I ever had!" It's like receiving a blue ribbon.

We home-school our girls, Sadie and Wren, and spend most days together—me greeting folks, Jamie running the kitchen, and the girls doing their homework at a corner table. People love seeing our family together. The girls jump in and help how they can. It's fun when they're around because people love talking to them, and they'll talk to anybody! They get to see what Mom and Dad love to do—work with people and good food.

People come to the Cafe for that good food, but they also come for the experience and fellowship, sitting on that iconic porch or sharing a table with someone they've never met. People drive an hour or more sometimes just to come to the Cafe. They say, "I get to eat good food, and we get to see each other."

Round Top is growing, and more restaurants have come to town, but people keep coming back to the Cafe. It's small and cozy. The ceilings are low. The lights are not super bright, and it has what Jamie calls "junk" all over the walls and ceiling—every piece a memory or patriotic memorabilia. A lot of restaurants are manufactured, but the Cafe has been cultivated over decades to be hospitable, friendly, warm, and welcoming.

You might come as a stranger, but you'll leave as a friend. The breakdowns we're seeing in our societies happen when relationships and love disintegrate. We want to love others as best we can. I always enjoy walking up to people in the Cafe or in their home for a Cooking Class or at a Wine Dinner—maybe someone I don't even know yet—and just striking up a conversation. It's meaningful for all of us. Listening to other people tells them you really do care. That's what people yearn for.

Building and serving communities has always been one of our purposes. We started a Pies for Purpose campaign a few years ago to help some organizations. When Hurricane Sandy hit in 2012, we drove a van full of donations—not just from the Cafe but also from our customers. That van was full of diapers, necessities, over $10,000 in gift cards, and pies. We did the same in Moore, Oklahoma, when the big tornado hit.

After Hurricane Ike in 2008, we donated food to the Salvation Army. During the COVID-19 pandemic, we set up drive-thrus at churches and gave 10 percent back. Kids got free lunches during the summer.

Over the years, we've expanded that idea of sharing food and fellowship through our catering business and our monthly Cooking Classes. We want people to know not just the joy of *eating* good food *with* friends and family, but also the joy of *cooking* good food *for* friends and family. I thought, "Wouldn't it be fun to do a cooking class and show people how to cook like we do at the Cafe?" So we do a cooking demonstration on site at the Cafe, in people's homes, and anywhere we're invited. Everybody gets a five-course meal and wine. Some folks are willing to fly halfway across the United States just to be in a Cooking Class.

We also started Wine Dinners, partnering with wineries and creating menus around the wines we love. Everyone gets three samples of the best wines, a bite to eat, and the option to buy incredible wines at a reasonable price. We beat all pricing. People love it! We realized that people really do care about cooking good food and sharing it with others.

Food is about taste, experience, and memories. It involves all your senses—what you smell, see, hear, taste, and even feel. And that all boils down to your heart. A good meal touches you because it's delicious, immersive, and memorable. It may even spark good memories. You want your friends and family leaving a meal saying, "Wow! That was a great experience." That's what great food, excellent service, and a good time will do.

Just make sure you know what the people you're cooking for like and don't like. The first three times the Alexander's had us over, they made salmon. After the third time, when we were driving home, I told JB, "Look, I've got to tell them that I can not stand salmon because I cannot force myself to eat it again." Our friends were pretty upset that we didn't tell them the first time!

Remember that people want their souls fed as much as their stomachs. We should deliver on those expectations.

That's what this cookbook is all about. So pour a glass of wine, and let's get cooking!

—————— JB & Jamie ——————

ENTERTAINMENT & APPETIZERS

I love appetizers because you get a little taste of everything. At Royers Cafe, the appetizers have the dynamic flavor that starts the meal off right, creating the memories and experience a good meal offers.

Appetizers and desserts are more important to me than the meal because they set and seal the expectations for the meal. If you have a great opening and ending to the experience—with a sub-par meal in between—you'll probably go back to that restaurant because you think, "Well, maybe I just ordered the wrong thing. I'll try something else next time." But if you have a bad appetizer and a bad dessert—even if the meal is fine—you probably won't go back.

Appetizers also make great icebreakers. When guests arrive, you can immediately start filling their stomachs as they wait for the meal—and no one is standing around feeling awkward. Just remember to plan the appetizers around the meal. If you're having Mexican or Tex-Mex, your appetizers could be chips with salsa, guacamole, or queso. If you're having burgers or steaks, try a charcuterie board, stuffed jalapeños, or buffalo wings. Italian? Make bruschetta—a favorite with our guests.

Jamie makes a baked brie wrapped in pastry dough and topped with honey, berries, and jalapeños. It's so good, it seems almost sinful! You eat all that gooey cheese, sweet honey, and tart berries on a salty cracker, and your mouth is loaded with so many levels of flavors. It's easy to make, and you can prepare it ahead of time so it comes out of the oven the moment your guests arrive.

Keeping the recipes simple but delicious is the key. You don't want them to be too complicated—just something fresh, easy, and ready to entice the taste buds. Since you eat with your eyes first, they should come out as pretty as they are good—and these recipes are just darn good!

If the food is great, you start talking and break that ice. And you're not just feeding a stomach—you're feeding a soul.

JB & Jamie

Jamie hates pimento, but loves this dip. It pairs with many food boards because the feta cheese gives it that salty flavor that blends well with cheddar cheese.

Bobbi's Pimento Cheese Dip

 Prep Time: 5 min

 Cook Time: 0 min

 Yields: 8–10 servings

Mix all ingredients together except mayonnaise.

Add mayonnaise and stir together. (We like to use our hands.)

Chill and serve with your favorite crackers or bread.

You can also spice it up by adding some of your own seasonings.

Highly Recommend: We love adding jalapeños and bacon.

4 cups sharp cheddar cheese, shredded

8 oz feta cheese, crumbled

1 tbsp Mrs. Dash

4 oz pimentos, drained

2 tsp mustard

2 cups mayonnaise

jalapeños (optional)

bacon, cooked (optional)

Serving Tip: crackers or bread

It's best made fresh, but you can also make it a day ahead. You can put it on a charcuterie board, serve it on a platter with crackers, plate it with fancy cut vegetables, or turn it into a killer grilled cheese! Because it's versatile, you can add bacon, jalapeños, chives, various cheeses, or whatever suits your fancy. Make it your own by creating different flavors that you like. At the Cafe, we serve this recipe with the Blue Cheese Dip as an appetizer.

JB & Jamie

ENTERTAINMENT & APPETIZERS

31

Tiny Cajun's Fried Green Tomatoes

Prep Time: 10 min   Cook Time: 5 min   Yields: 6–8 servings

Prepare two bowls:

Bowl 1 (Dry): Mix together 1 tbsp Tony Seasoning, 1 tbsp garlic powder, 1 tbsp black pepper, and cornmeal.

Bowl 2 (Wet): Beat eggs and season liberally with remaining Tony Seasoning, garlic, and pepper.

Slice tomatoes 1/4" thick.

Heat oil in frying pan.

Dip tomato slices into dry mixture, then dip into wet mixture, then dip back into dry mixture.

Place tomato slices into heated oil and cook a couple minutes per side.

Place a bed of lettuce on your serving dish and scoop spoonfuls of Bobbi's Pimento Cheese Dip down the center of the plate.

Top with fried green tomatoes and a drizzle of Royers Creamy Cajun Sauce.

2 tbsp Tony Chachere's Creole Seasoning

2 tbsp garlic powder

2 tbsp coarse black pepper

2 cups cornmeal

3 eggs

4 whole green tomatoes

vegetable oil

lettuce (for plating)

Bobbi's Pimento Cheese Dip (p. 31)

Royers Creamy Cajun Sauce (p. 247)

Since Jamie's from Louisiana, she likes to bring Cajun flare to the menu. Lots of seasoning and cornmeal make them pop in your mouth!

— JB & Jamie —

ENTERTAINMENT & APPETIZERS

Bacon Wrapped Lamb Lollipops

Prep Time: 10 min

Cook Time: 10 min

Yields: 3–4 servings

Cut rack of lamb into individual lollipops.

Season lamb with Royers Grilling Seasoning and wrap with bacon.

Put a toothpick through the bacon and lamb to hold them in place.

Heat oil in frying pan.

On medium high heat, lightly fry lollipops in oil on each side until bacon is fully cooked.

Remove toothpicks before serving.

Use our Lemon Garlic Basil Sauce for dipping.

1 rack of lamb

8–10 slices bacon

Royers Grilling Seasoning (P.259)

about an inch of vegetable oil in a pan

Lemon Garlic Basil Sauce (p. 254)

These are perfect for parties and appetizers, even if you're not a lamb fan.

JB & Jamie

Chili Lime Shrimp Tostada

Prep Time: 20 min

Cook Time: 5 min

Yields: 6–8 servings

Heat a thin layer of Royers Dill Butter in a medium-sized cast iron skillet.

Add shrimp to skillet and season with Royers Grilling Seasoning.

When the shrimp are cooked, lay them on a paper towel to dry.

In a bowl, combine shrimp, corn, tomatoes, and onion. Mix well.

Combine all ingredients for the dressing. Blend well.

Pour the dressing over the shrimp mixture. Stir.

Fry the tortillas until crisp.

Dollop 1 tbsp guacamole onto each tortilla.

Top with shrimp mixture.

Garnish with cilantro and cotija cheese.

Royers Dill Butter (p. 256)

1 lb shrimp

Royers Grilling Seasoning (p. 259)

1/2 cup frozen corn, thawed

1 cup cherry tomatoes, diced

1/4 cup red onion, diced

1/2 cup guacamole

corn tortillas, street taco size

cilantro (optional)

cotija cheese (optional)

Dressing

3 tbsp lime juice

2 tbsp oil (avocado or olive)

3 tsp chili powder

1 tsp onion powder

1/2 tsp salt

We just started making these at the Cafe as part of a dinner special. They're fresh, crispy, and pair well with the guacamole.

JB & Jamie

Royers Baked Brie

 Prep Time: 15 min   **Cook Time: 40 min**   **Yields: 4–6 servings**

Preheat oven to 400°F.

Cut the rind off the brie.

Sprinkle flour on your countertop and roll out puff pastry.

Place brie in puff pastry and wrap it up like a yummy little gift.

Bake in 400°F oven for 30–40 minutes or until pastry is golden brown.

In a small pot on the stove, mix together blueberries, jalapeños, honey, and sugar on medium heat until mixed together like a sauce.

Place baked brie on a platter and top with the blueberry sauce.

Serve with crackers or warm French bread.

1 wheel of brie

puff pastry*

1 cup frozen or fresh blueberries

2 tbsp jalapeños, diced

1/4 cup honey

1/4 cup sugar

Serving Tip: crackers or french bread

* Find puff pastries in the freezer section of your grocery store.

This appetizer makes a great opening for our Wine Dinners. The flavors of the melted brie, blueberries, jalapeños, and honey on a salty cracker pair well with white wine. You can shake it up and try vegetables or various fruits. It's hands down a home-run dish.

JB & Jamie

Cafe's Blue Cheese Dip

Prep Time: 40 min

Cook Time: 0 min

Yields: 6–8 servings

Combine blue cheese, garlic, and olive oil.

Spread mixture onto bottom of a dish.

Mix red wine vinegar, lemon juice, red onion, and cilantro.

Pour on top of blue cheese mixture.

For best flavor, refrigerate at least 30 minutes.

Serve with crackers or warm French bread (or use as a topping for your favorite sandwich or burger).

12 oz blue cheese, crumbled

3 tbsp garlic, minced

1/3 cup olive oil

4 tbsp red wine vinegar

2 tbsp lemon juice

1 cup red onion, chopped

1 cup cilantro, minced

Serving Tip: crackers or french bread

People who don't like blue cheese (including Jamie!) love this dip!

The vinegar in the marinade cuts the pungency of the blue cheese. It's a universal dip that I put on everything—great on a burger, killer on a filet. The color makes it beautiful on a charcuterie board.

— JB & Jamie —

Pulled Pork Tacos

Prep Time: 10 min

Cook Time: 8 hours

Yields: 4–6 servings

Rinse pork in sink. Set aside.

Mix salt, pepper, paprika, and garlic powder in a bowl.

Roll pork in seasoning mixture.

Place in crock-pot with diced onion, garlic cloves, and fresh orange juice.

Cook on low for 8 hours or medium-low for 4–6 hours.

Shred with fork.

Serve on your favorite tortillas with rice and preferred toppings.

Top with Royers Cilantro Ranch Dressing.

2 lb pork shoulder

2 tsp pink salt

1 tsp black pepper

2 tsp paprika

1 tsp garlic powder

1/2 yellow onion, diced

4 cloves garlic

juice of 1 orange

corn or flour tortillas, street taco size

rice, prepared

Royers Cilantro Ranch Dressing (p. 249)

People love tiny tacos. They are easy and stress free and seem to set people at ease in gatherings. So when you make them delicious they become the perfect appetizer to set the mood for a for a fun evening with friends. You can serve them fancy with perfect garnishes or you can set them out deconstructed in a "craft your own" style to get the conversations started at your next gathering.

JB & Jamie

ENTERTAINMENT & APPETIZERS

Balsamic Caprese Skewers

Prep Time: 10 min   Cook Time: 0 min   Yields: 8–10 servings

1 package fresh mozzarella, sliced

1 container cherry tomatoes

1 bunch basil

balsamic reduction*

1 package fun party picks

*Find balsamic reduction in the salad dressing aisle at your local grocery store

Cut mozzarella slices in quarters.

Layer the mozzarella, tomatoes, and basil by skewering on toothpicks (see picture).

Display skewers on your favorite platter.

Drizzle with balsamic reduction.

This one is easy, fun, and yummy! It's perfect for a party or event. This simple recipe can be made ahead of time so you can enjoy the fun.

Kids love helping put this one together too!

— JB & Jamie —

Sadie's Bruschetta

Prep Time: 40 min   **Cook Time:** 5 min   **Yields:** 8–10 servings

Mix together tomato, onion, basil, garlic, and salt.

Let mixture marinate in the refrigerator for at least 30 minutes (we recommend 1 hour or more) to bring out the best flavor.

Spread a little olive oil on slices of French bread.

Toast bread and cut into squares.

Place toasted bread on a platter and top with mozzarella.

Top with a spoonful of tomato mixture and drizzle with balsamic reduction.

1 large tomato, diced

1/2 red onion, diced

10 basil leaves, chopped

1 heaping tbsp garlic, minced

sprinkle of salt

olive oil

1 loaf French bread, sliced

1 log fresh sliced mozzarella

balsamic reduction*

*Find balsamic reduction in the salad dressing aisle at your local grocery store

This is Sadie's favorite. It's best to let the tomato, onions, and basil marinate with the salt and garlic to get those flavors mixed together. Serving it with crusty French bread gives it a nice crunch. At the Cafe we also spice it up a bit by using a jalapeño hoagie instead of the french loaf!

JB & Jamie

Lamb and Feta Sliders with Chimichurri

 Prep Time: 15 min

 Cook Time: 10 min

 Yields: 4–5 servings

Mix lamb and seasoning in a bowl.

Form lamb into 3 oz patties.

Grill patties on a flat top grill or cast iron skillet on the stove (a couple minutes on each side).

Toast slider buns while patties are cooking.

Place patties on bottom toasted bun.

Add a spoonful of Chimichurri Sauce and feta cheese to each slider.

Cap with the top bun and serve!

1 lb lamb, ground

Royers Grilling Seasoning (p. 259)

slider buns

Chimichurri Sauce (p. 253)

8 oz feta cheese, crumbled

These are sure to be a crowd pleaser! This is an unexpected mouthwatering menu item that we bring to our Cooking Classes because we get so many requests to learn how to make it! The Chimichurri Sauce combined with the saltiness of the feta cheese is incredible.

— JB & Jamie —

JB & Jamie

Best deviled eggs! An unexpected twist on a classic makes these deviled eggs a fan favorite! We serves these at our Cooking Class and many of our Caterings.

They look amazing on a Charcuterie Board!

Deviled Eggs with Avocado and Bacon

 **Prep Time: 30 min**   **Cook Time: 25 min** **Yields: 10–12 servings**

Boil eggs for 12 minutes. Turn off burner and cover pot for 15 minutes.

Fry bacon and set aside.

Drain water from the eggs and place them in a bowl with ice cold water for a few minutes before peeling.

Peel eggs and cut in half.

Set the halved whites upright on a plate (ready to be filled) and place the yolks in a bowl.

Mash yolks.

Add avocado, salt, pepper, mayonnaise, and mustard to the mashed yolks. Mix well.

Once it is mixed well (creamy-like texture), put in a zip-top bag. Clip the corner of the zip-top bag to allow you to pipe the mixture into the egg halves.

Top with chopped bacon pieces and garnish with paprika.

1 dozen eggs

8 slices bacon, fried and chopped

2 large avocados

1/4 tsp pink salt

1 tsp black pepper

2/3 cup mayonnaise

2 tbsp mustard

paprika (optional)

The easiest way I have found to peel eggs is to place them in a Mason jar and give them a good shake. The shells come right off (usually).

JB & Jamie

SALADS & SIDES

Great sides elevate the whole meal experience. When you think of Texas, you think of barbecue. A lot of places have great barbecue but horrible sides. At Royers Cafe, you're never going to get horrible. All the sides are made from scratch, originating from home recipes we've tweaked into even greater goodness. The fresh ingredients and spices make these sides a winner, not only at the Cafe but also at our Wine Dinners and Cooking Classes.

Good sides should bring you back home, reminding you of good meals eaten around the family table. A lot of these sides are recipes we grew up eating, and there are precious family stories behind them. As you make the sides in this cookbook and modify them to suit your tastes, you'll start creating memories for your own friends and family.

One of the best parts of our side dishes is that many of them are strong enough to stand alone without a heavy meat dish. Take for instance our Jalapeño Cheese Grits. They can be served as a perfect side dish to any number of main courses, but if you toss on a few grilled shrimp—Bam! They become a visually stunning and memorable main course. It is all about presentation and the flavors you want to spotlight.

An important thing we have always kept in mind when creating our recipes was to keep them simple while maintaining a powerful taste. So next time you are invited to a potluck family gathering and you need to bring a side dish, you can wow them with a simple recipe that will entice the taste buds and upstage any other course.

Shrimp BLT Salad

 Prep Time: 10 min   **Cook Time: 10 min**   **Yields: 2 servings**

Heat a thin layer of Royers Dill Butter in a medium-sized cast iron skillet.

Add shrimp to skillet and season with Royers Grilling Seasoning.

When the shrimp are cooked, lay them on a paper towel to dry.

Cook bacon in skillet until slices are nice and crispy. Then lay bacon on paper towel to dry.

Assemble salad using remaining ingredients.

Top salad with shrimp and bacon.

Toast french bread and chop into squares to make a crunchy croutons.

Royers Dill Butter (p. 256)

1 lb Gulf shrimp

Royers Grilling Seasoning (p. 259)

5 slices thick-cut bacon

1 bag spring mix

1/2 red onion, sliced

10 cherry tomatoes, sliced

balsamic dressing

toasted french bread (optional)

The Shrimp BLT is one of the most ordered sandwiches at the Cafe, so we knew that the salad would be a hit. We were not wrong. The flavors of the shrimp pop on the greens with the zing of the dressing.

JB & Jamie

SALADS & SIDES

Strawberry Goat Cheese Salad

 Prep Time: 8 min

 Cook Time: 5 min

 Yields: 2 servings

Slice strawberries.

Toast pecans in skillet (no need to add oil; pecans will release enough oil, but make sure you are watching these, stirring frequently to prevent burning).

Place spring mix in serving dishes.

Top with strawberries, toasted pecans, and goat cheese.

Drizzle with balsamic reduction.

Add grilled chicken if you want to eat it as a meal.

10 strawberries

1 cup pecan pieces

1 bag spring mix

8 oz goat cheese, crumbled

balsamic reduction*

grilled chicken (optional)

*Find balsamic reduction in the salad dressing aisle at your local grocery store

This is great for a hot summer day. We start off a lot of Wine Dinners with this salad because it pairs well with rosé, sparkling wine, champagne, or prosecco. It's a popular summertime salad.

JB & Jamie

Royers Waldorf Salad

 Prep Time: 8 min

 Cook Time: 5 min

 Yields: 2 servings

Slice apple and onion.

Toast pecans in skillet (no need to add oil; pecans will release enough oil, but make sure you are watching these, stirring frequently to prevent burning).

Place spring mix in serving dishes.

Top with apples, onions, pecans, and blue cheese.

Drizzle with balsamic reduction.

Add grilled chicken if you want to eat it as a meal.

1 green apple

1/2 red onion

1 cup pecans

1 bag spring mix

8 oz blue cheese, crumbled

balsamic reduction*

grilled chicken (optional)

*Find balsamic reduction in the salad dressing aisle at your local grocery store

I love this salad because it has blue cheese. Anytime you put blue cheese on anything, you elevate it. The apples add a crisp freshness and make it a great pick for a hot summer day!

— JB & Jamie —

SALADS & SIDES

Bud's Salad

Prep Time: 20 min   Cook Time: 15 min   Yields: 2 servings

Cover cast iron skillet with Royers Dill Butter.

Royers Dill Butter (p. 256)

Once it's piping hot, place beef tenderloin in the skillet.

1 lb beef tenderloin, cubed

Sprinkle heavily with Royers Grilling Seasoning.

Royers Grilling Seasoning (p. 259)

Cook to preference.

5 slices thick-sliced bacon

While beef is cooking, fry strips of bacon (not too crisp).

1 bag spring mix

Place spring mix in serving dishes.

1 red onion, sliced

Add onions, tomatoes, and Royers Blue Cheese Dressing.

1 cup cherry tomatoes, halved

Add cooked beef tenderloin and bacon.

Royers Blue Cheese Dressing (p. 246)

Top with blue cheese crumbles.

1/2 cup blue cheese, crumbled

Bacon, beef, blue cheese—what could go wrong?

JB & Jamie

Grandma Kay's German Potato Salad

Prep Time: 10 min

Cook Time: 20 min

Yields: 5–6 servings

Dice potatoes and cook for 20 minutes in boiling water.

Combine remaining ingredients in a large bowl.

Drain potatoes.

Mix potatoes with ingredients in bowl.

Serve warm.

- 2 lbs red potatoes
- 1 cup mayonnaise
- 1/4 cup Dijon mustard
- 1/2 cup red onion, chopped
- 2 green onions, chopped
- 2 garlic cloves, minced
- 1 tbsp dry dill
- 1/2 tsp salt (add more as needed)
- 1/2 tsp pepper (add more as needed)

This recipe is inspired by our neighbor, Grandma Kay.

This recipe is intended to be served warm, but it can also be served chilled. We have so many friends who love it both ways. Feel free to serve it to your guests the way you love it!

JB & Jamie

SALADS & SIDES

Baked Potato Salad

 Prep Time: 10 min   **Cook Time: 20 min**   **Yields: 5–6 servings**

Dice potatoes and cook for 20 minutes in boiling water.

3 lbs potatoes, peeled

Drain potatoes.

8 tbsp (1 stick) butter, softened

Place potatoes back in pot and give them a rough mash.

1 cup sour cream

Stir in butter, sour cream, salt, and pepper to taste.

salt

pepper

Place potatoes in serving bowl.

1 bunch green onions, chopped

Place in refrigerator to chill until ready to serve.

6 slices bacon, cooked and chopped

Top with green onions, bacon, and cheese.

1 cup cheddar cheese, shredded

The perfect cold potato salad that goes great with fried chicken.

— JB & Jamie —

SALADS & SIDES

JB & Jamie

We introduced this chicken salad during the COVID-19 pandemic. We were serving our Royers Sunday Fried Chicken, drive-thru style, and had some leftovers. We marinate our chicken for 24 hours and it has a ton of flavor and we didn't want it to go to waste, so we deboned it and turned it into Buffalo Chicken Salad. Now we have regulars who beg us to make it!

Buffalo Chicken Salad

Prep Time: 30 min

Cook Time: 15 min

Yields: 5–6 servings

You can use grilled or fried chicken for this recipe. If you are grilling, get a skillet hot, season chicken with salt and pepper, and cook on both sides until fully cooked.

Dice cooked chicken and put in a large mixing bowl.

Add mayonnaise, sour cream, and onions. Mix.

Add Frank's RedHot and more salt and pepper to taste. (If you want to start with a little less Frank's, that is fine too! You can always add, but you can't take away!)

Refrigerate until chilled.

Eat with crackers or on your favorite bread.

Highly Recommend: Add a little blue cheese and bacon to the mixture.

2 lbs chicken

salt

pepper

1/2 cup mayonnaise

1 cup sour cream

1/2 red onion, chopped

1 bunch green onion, chopped (less if you aren't a fan)

1/2 cup Frank's RedHot

crackers or bread

blue cheese crumbles (optional)

bacon, cooked (optional)

You can use grilled or fried chicken for this recipe. We use our leftover Royers Sunday Fried Chicken (p. 157)

JB & Jamie

Lavender Chicken Salad

Prep Time: 30 min

Cook Time: 15 min

Yields: 5–6 servings

2 lbs chicken

1/4 cup chives, chopped

1 1/2 tbsp lavender

zest of 1 lemon

juice of 1/2 lemon

1/4 cup red onion, diced

1/2 cup mayonnaise

1 cup Greek yogurt

1 tsp salt

2 tsp extra virgin olive oil

1/2 cup pistachios, chopped

1 tbsp coarse ground pepper

sprinkle of Tony Chachere's Creole Seasoning

Grill chicken with salt and pepper.

After grilling the chicken, dice it.

Combine the rest of the ingredients and mix with the chicken.

Refrigerate until chilled to get the best flavor.

We'll admit that Lavender Chicken Salad doesn't sound like it would be good. Trust us. It's tasty.

JB & Jamie

SALADS & SIDES

Watermelon Feta Salad

Prep Time: 10 min   **Cook Time:** 0 min   **Yields:** 5–6 servings

Mix all ingredients together in a bowl.

Chill and serve.

- 6 cups watermelon, cubed
- 1 small container blueberries
- 1/2 red onion, diced
- 8 oz feta, crumbled
- 1/4–1/2 cup chopped mint
- 1 tbsp olive oil
- juice of 1/2 lemon
- pinch of salt

The key to this salad is making it ahead of time to allow the flavors to come together. It is a great mix of flavors and amazingly refreshing on a hot summer day!

JB & Jamie

Quinoa Salad

 Prep Time: 10 min   **Cook Time: 20 min**   **Yields: 5–6 servings**

Boil quinoa as directed.

Place in fridge or freezer until cooled.

Add remaining ingredients and mix well.

Serve cold.

1 12-oz box quinoa (can be tricolored, red, or white)

1 cup Lemon Garlic Basil Sauce (p. 254)

1/4 cup olive oil

1/4 cup fresh basil, chopped

1/2 cup dried cranberries

8 oz feta cheese, crumbled

salt

pepper

This is Jamie's favorite salad at the Cafe!

JB & Jamie

SALADS & SIDES

Royers Cold Broccoli Salad

Prep Time: 5 min

Cook Time: 2 min

Yields: 5–6 servings

Blanch broccoli.

Chop broccoli in bite size pieces.

Combine onion, mayonnaise, sugar, and raisins.

Add broccoli to mayonnaise mixture.

Add bacon, sunflower seeds, or golden raisins for added flavor and texture.

Refrigerate.

Serve cold.

2 lbs broccoli

1/2 red onion, chopped

1 cup mayonnaise

1/3 cup sugar

1/2 cup raisins

bacon, sunflower seeds, golden raisins (optional)

This salad has been around since 1987.
It's a staple at the Cafe and everyone loves it.

JB & Jamie

Colorful Cold Corn Medley

Prep Time: 15 min   Cook Time: 5 min   Yields: 4–5 servings

In large saucepan, bring 2 inches of water to a boil.

Stir in sugar.

Add corn and continue to boil for 5 minutes.

Remove from heat.

Drain and let corn cool.

Add red pepper, green peppers, onion, Monterey Jack cheese, and olive oil.

Mix well.

Season with cumin, cayenne pepper, salt, and pepper to taste.

- 1/2 tsp sugar
- 1 lb frozen corn
- 1 large red bell pepper, chopped
- 2 large green peppers, chopped
- 1 medium red onion, chopped
- 8 oz Monterey Jack cheese, cubed
- 1 tbsp olive oil
- ground cumin
- cayenne pepper
- salt
- pepper

This is a colorful, beautiful salad that we use for catered events.

JB & Jamie

Parmesan Lemon Asparagus

 Prep Time: 5 min

 Cook Time: 5 min

 Yields: 3–4 servings

Cut ends off of asparagus and place in a large pan on the stove (cast iron works great).

Lightly coat with olive oil, salt, and pepper.

Cook, stirring/turning asparagus until tender.

Add lemon juice.

Sprinkle with Parmesan cheese.

Serve (or just eat it right out of the pan)!

1 bundle asparagus

olive oil

salt

pepper

juice of 1 lemon

freshly grated Parmesan cheese

This is a Wine Dinner staple that goes great with any meat.

JB & Jamie

Maque Choux

Prep Time: 20 min

Cook Time: 30 min

Yields: 5–6 servings

In a large skillet, heat oil over medium heat.

Add onions and bell peppers, cooking until onions are translucent.

Stir in garlic. Cook for additional minute.

Add corn.

Season to taste with salt and pepper. Add cayenne for a kick.

Cook 1–2 minutes.

Pour in cream and bring to a boil.

Reduce heat. Simmer until cream reduces and thickens slightly (approx. 5 minutes).

Pour into a serving dish.

Garnish with red and green bell peppers.

1 tbsp olive oil

1/2 sweet onion, chopped

1/2 green bell pepper, chopped

1/2 red bell pepper, chopped

1 tbsp garlic, minced

12 oz frozen corn

salt

pepper

pinch of cayenne (optional)

1/2 cup heavy cream

This is a huge hit at our Cajun Cooking Class. It's JB's favorite corn dish. It is a fun dish to serve to guests because it tastes amazing but it is also beautiful!

JB & Jamie

SALADS & SIDES

Jan's Baked Beans

Prep Time: 10 min

Cook Time: 1–1.5 hours

Yields: 8–10 servings

Pour the pork and beans into an 11" x 13" baking pan.

In a bowl, combine ketchup, mustard, and brown sugar. Mix until a smooth consistency.

Add mixture to the beans.

Add green onions and bacon.

Bake at 350° for 1–1 1/2 hours.

2 28-oz cans baked beans

2 cups ketchup

1/4 cup mustard

1 cup brown sugar

1 bunch of green onions, chopped

4 slices of uncooked bacon, cut into 1" pieces

A perfect side for barbecue and a frequent catering order.

JB & Jamie

SALADS & SIDES

JB & Jamie

Remember, you can add salt, but you can't take it away!

Garlic Mashed Potatoes

Prep Time: 5 min

Cook Time: 25 min

Yields: 10–12 servings

Instructions	Ingredients
Peel and dice potatoes.	3 lbs potatoes
Place potatoes in a pot with water and boil until fork tender.	8 tbsp (1 stick) butter
Drain potatoes.	1/2 cup milk
Use electric mixer to whip potatoes.	3 cloves garlic, minced
Add butter, milk, garlic, salt, and pepper. Mix a few more minutes until well blended.	salt
	pepper

These are a staple at Wine Dinners and Cooking Classes.

Be sure to use fresh garlic.
JB says the more garlic, the better!

— JB & Jamie —

SALADS & SIDES

Royers Creamed Corn

Prep Time: 5 min

Cook Time: 15 min

Yields: 4–6 servings

Cook frozen corn per package instructions. Drain water.

Heat creamed corn in microwave and combine with cooked frozen corn.

In a pan, melt butter.

Add cream cheese chunks. Stir until melted.

Add corn mixture to butter/cream cheese mixture.

Add salt and pepper to taste.

Continue to stir until well mixed and hot throughout.

16 oz frozen corn

14–16 oz can creamed corn

16 tbsp (2 sticks) butter

8 oz cream cheese, cut into chunks

salt

pepper

We serve this side with our Sunday Fried Chicken. It's easy to make, and everyone loves it.

JB & Jamie

Sweet Potato Casserole

Prep Time: 20 min

Cook Time: 45 min

Yields: 8–10 servings

Preheat oven to 350°F.

Mash sweet potatoes in mixing bowl.

Add 3/4 cup of the butter, sugar, eggs, and vanilla. Mix until smooth.

Pour into a 9" x 13" casserole dish.

Mix coconut, brown sugar, remaining butter (1/2 cup), pecans, and flour.

Spread mix over sweet potatoes.

Bake for 30–45 minutes, until topping browns.

60 oz canned sweet potatoes, drained (not mashed)

1 1/4 cups butter, melted

1 cup sugar

2 eggs

1 tsp vanilla

1 cup shredded coconut

1 cup brown sugar, packed

1 cup pecans, chopped

2 tbsp flour

JB's mom made this when he was a kid.
It's like a dessert.

JB & Jamie

SALADS & SIDES

Granny's Cornbread Dressing

Prep Time: 45 min   **Cook Time: 50–60 min**   **Yields: 6–8 servings**

Preheat oven to 350°F.

Melt butter in skillet.

Add onion and celery.
Cook until soft but not browned.
Remove from heat and set aside.

Mix remaining ingredients.

Add onion/celery mixture.

Add enough chicken stock
to moisten.

Pour into casserole dish.

Cover and bake for 50–60 minutes.

*If you prefer walnuts - they are an easy
substitute for the pecans. (In fact, they were
in the original recipe!) At the Cafe, we love
the taste that the pecans bring and have
enjoyed using them over the years!

8 tbsp (1 stick) butter

1 cup onion, chopped

1 cup celery, chopped

2 large eggs

6 cups toasted bread, cubed

2 8.5-oz packages cornbread mix, prepared per package instructions, chunked/cubed

1/2 cup pecans*, coarsely chopped

1 tbsp poultry seasoning

1 tsp salt

1 tsp pepper

4 cups (approx.) chicken stock

This was JB's grandma's (Granny Wofford's) recipe, and everyone loves it. Jamie never liked cornbread stuffing until she had this one. It has nuts in it, which seems odd, but it gives it a good texture. Just don't overcook it because it will dry out.

JB & Jamie

SALADS & SIDES

JB & Jamie

Our Jalapeño Cheese Grits are one of our top selling sides of all times! These grits are going to blow your mind.

Jalapeño Cheese Grits

Prep Time: 10 min **Cook Time: 30 min** **Yields: 6-8 servings**

Boil 4 1/2 cups water.

Add jalapeños, garlic, paprika, cayenne, salt, and butter.

Return to boil, add grits.

Whisk until all water is absorbed.

Turn off heat and cover for 5 minutes.

Add eggs (be sure to constantly stir so they do not scramble).

Add cream cheese. Mix.

Add pepper jack cheese, American cheese, heavy whipping cream and water (up to 2 additional cups when you need more liquid).

4 1/2 cups water

2 tbsp jalapeños, chopped

2 tbsp garlic, minced

1/2 tsp paprika

1/2 tsp cayenne

1 tbsp salt

8 tbsp (1 stick) butter

12 oz quick grits

3 eggs

4 oz cream cheese

16 oz Pepper Jack cheese

12 oz American cheese

1/2 qt heavy whipping cream

1 1/2—2 cups water

We went to Savannah, Georgia, and everyone was like, "Get the grits." JB said, "No, I don't have to because I know where the best grits are."

JB & Jamie

Coach's Green Beans

 Prep Time: 10 min   Cook Time: 30–40 min   Yields: 7–8 servings

Take 7 frozen green beans, and wrap them in bacon.

Lightly spray casserole dish with cooking spray.

Place bacon-wrapped green beans in a casserole dish with the end of the bacon at the bottom.

Mix together butter, brown sugar, soy sauce, and garlic salt.

Drizzle over green bean bundles.

Bake in 350°F oven 30–40 minutes or until bacon looks cooked.

2 bags frozen cut green beans

1 lb bacon, sliced in half

8 tbsp (1 stick) butter, melted

1 cup brown sugar

2 tbsp soy sauce

1 tsp garlic salt

This recipe is delicious and simple.

It will steal the show at Thanksgiving.

— JB & Jamie —

SALADS & SIDES

Creamy Three-Cheese Macaroni

Prep Time: 10 min

Cook Time: 15 min

Yields: 3–4 servings

Cook your favorite pasta, and drain.

In a separate pot, combine butter, rosemary, and minced garlic.

Add heavy whipping cream, and bring to a boil.

Start adding cheeses while stirring or whisking constantly so the cheeses don't burn.

Once all cheeses are fully melted into a sauce, add the cheese sauce to the pasta.

Stir together and garnish with extra shredded cheese and parsley.

- 1 lb of your favorite pasta
- 8 tbsp (1 stick) butter
- 1 sprig rosemary, minced
- 2 cloves garlic, minced
- 2–3 cups heavy whipping cream
- 8 oz cheddar cheese, shredded
- 8 oz American cheese
- 8 oz grated Parmesan cheese
- parsley (optional)

We never bake our macaroni. Baking dries it out! This recipe is a creamy blend of butter, heavy whipping cream, cheddar cheese, American cheese, and Parmesan cheese.

JB & Jamie

SALADS & SIDES

Fried Brussels Sprouts

 Prep Time: 10 min

 Cook Time: 10 min

 Yields: 5–6 servings

In a cast iron skillet, heat half an inch of oil until hot.

Cut off ends of brussels sprouts, and put in oil, frying lightly.

(Don't worry if some of the leaves fall off - that makes them crispy and yummy!)

When the brussels sprouts are light golden brown, place them on a paper-towel-lined cookie sheet to drain excess grease.

Combine honey, Sriracha, soy sauce, and lemon juice.

Pour mixture over brussels sprouts and toss.

vegetable oil

1 lb brussels sprouts

1/4 cup honey

1/4 cup Sriracha

1 tbsp soy sauce

splash of lemon juice

We made these at a Cooking Class, and everyone agreed they were the best brussels sprouts.

The sweet-and-spicy kick brings them to life.

JB & Jamie

Mashed Potato Casserole

 Prep Time: 20 min

 Cook Time: 25 min

 Yields: 8–10 servings

Preheat oven to 350°F.

Peel and slice potatoes about 1/4 inch thick.

Boil potatoes until soft (approx 10 minutes). Drain water.

Add seasoning, and mash with a potato masher. Use a hand mixer for creamier potatoes.

Add sour cream, butter, salt, and pepper to taste.

Place potatoes in a casserole dish. Cook potatoes 15 minutes or until warm.

Top with shredded cheddar cheese or blue cheese crumbles and bacon.

5 lbs Yukon gold potatoes

2 oz ranch dressing mix

16 oz sour cream

16 tbsp (2 sticks) butter, softened

salt

pepper

shredded cheddar cheese or blue cheese crumbles

bacon

These are one of the Cafe's most-ordered sides. There are a million ways to make potatoes, but the key is to whip them. The kind of potato you use can make all the difference. We like Yukon golds, but some people like russet or red. The trick is to boil them only until they're fork-tender and then mix them until fluffy. If you let them sit in water too long or mix them too long, they will become gummy from all the starch.

JB & Jamie

JB & Jamie

A great fall dish loaded with butter, cheese, and jalapeños.
This dish will warm you right up!

Cheesy Squash Casserole

Prep Time: 10 min

Cook Time: 20 min

Yields: 6–8 servings

Melt butter in pan and sauté onions.

Once onions are translucent, add squash, garlic, jalapeños, and heavy whipping cream.

Bring to a boil.

Slowly add cheese while stirring.

Once cheese is melted, add salt pepper and Tony Chachere's Creole Seasoning to taste.

4 lbs yellow squash, sliced

4 tbsp butter

1 red onion, chopped

2 tbsp garlic, minced

2–4 tbsp jalapeños, chopped

1 pint heavy whipping cream

1 lb American cheese

salt

pepper

Tony Chachere's Creole Seasoning

If you need to, you can use frozen squash. Just be sure to bring the frozen squash to room temperature before starting.

JB & Jamie

SALADS & SIDES

Slow Cooker Red Beans and Rice

 Prep Time: 10 min   **Cook Time:** 10 hours   **Yields:** 8–10 servings

Put beans, sausage, onion, and Tony Chachere's Creole Seasoning in crock-pot. Cover with water.

Cook overnight (10 hours) on low.

Remove a small bowl of the beans and mash with a fork. Add back to beans to thicken them.

Serve over your favorite rice.

2 lb small red beans

2 12-oz packages sausage (we use beef), sliced

1 yellow onion, chopped

2 tbsp Tony Chachere's Creole Seasoning

1 tsp salt

1 tsp pepper

Serving Tip: rice, prepared

So simple but so darn good! One of our favorite family dishes! Perfect cold-weather dish.

JB & Jamie

SALADS & SIDES

SOUPS & SANDWICHES

Soup is a well-known comfort food. When it's cold, you want soup. If you don't feel well, you want soup. It kind of reminds you of Mom's cooking and special care, bringing a memory of home to any meal.

Our Jalapeño Cheese Soup does just that for me. When my family first moved to Round Top, we lived in a rental house that was so cold we could feel the wind blowing through the walls. So we made this soup, hot and creamy with a little kick. It's just delicious. We have served it since the winter of '87 and it continues to be one of our top sellers.

The same is true of sandwiches—they're the lunches of childhood! They can be comforting, delicious, fun, and great for parties. The great thing about them is that you can capture a lot of flavor in just a few simple ingredients and with a few tips and tricks, you can produce a restaurant-quality sandwich in any home kitchen. You can get creative by trying various sauces, meats, toppings, and fresh ingredients. You don't like a regular burger bun? Try ciabatta or pretzel buns. There's no wrong way to make a sandwich.

And the best part about sandwiches is that they can be elevated and paired with soups or served alone for a light option. All you have to do is think of the event you are hosting or the guests that are coming over. Is it fancy? Serve the soup and sandwiches on matching plates and slice up some beautiful garnishes to place on top of the soup or the side of the plates. Honestly just a sprig of parsley and a few slices of a pepper step up the class level quite a bit. Is it casual? Grab some paper towels and a picnic basket and don't stress!

Creamy Tomato Basil Soup

Prep Time: 10 min   Cook Time: 45 min   Yields: 6–8 servings

Place onion, basil, garlic, olive oil, in large pot. Cook until onions are translucent. Be careful not to burn the garlic.

Add remaining ingredients, and bring to a boil.

Let simmer 20 minutes, stirring occasionally.

Add salt and pepper to taste.

1 yellow onion, diced

1 package basil, diced

2 tbsp garlic, chopped

1 tbsp olive oil

1 large can tomato soup

2 cups water

1 large can diced tomatoes (pulse about 10 times in blender)

1 jar marinara

1 pint heavy whipping cream

salt

pepper

This soup is another staple at the Cafe. When our first baby, Sadie, was born, we had about $10 in the bank. So we made tomato basil soup and grilled cheese sandwiches. Now at the Cafe, we serve this soup with a grilled cheese sandwich made with our Bobbi's Pimento Cheese Dip. It's a perfect combo.

JB & Jamie

SOUPS & SANDWICHES

JB & Jamie

It kind of looks like baby food, but it's delicious. It's sweet potatoes, squash, mushrooms, zucchini, and spices all cooked down. You've got to try it to believe it. Sprinkle some feta cheese on top, and dive in!

Sweet Potato Soup

Prep Time: 20 min   Cook Time: 20 min   Yields: 6–8 servings

Sauté onions and garlic in olive oil until onions are translucent.

Add squash and mushroom, and sauté a few more minutes.

Add chicken broth and all seasonings.

Add puréed sweet potatoes. Stir well.

Add heavy whipping cream, and bring to a simmer.

Add cilantro at the end when removing from heat.

1/2 red onion, diced

2 cloves garlic, chopped

2 tbsp olive oil

1 squash, sliced

1 portabella mushroom, sliced

2 cups chicken broth

1 tsp cumin

1 tsp chili powder

2 tsp salt

2 tsp Seasoned Salt

1 tsp black pepper

60 oz canned sweet potatoes, puréed

1 cup heavy whipping cream

1/2 bunch cilantro, chopped

You can simplify this recipe by using a pre-made roux from your local grocery store!

Maw Maw's Cajun Gumbo

Prep Time: 1 hour

Cook Time: 3 hours

Yields: A LOT!

ROUX

Heat oil. Gradually add flour until the consistency and color is that of a chocolate cake mix.

Set the roux aside.

GUMBO GRAVY

In a large gumbo pot, fill it a little more than halfway with water.

Add green onions, yellow onion, and seasonings to desired taste.

Bring to a boil.

Then add the roux a little at a time until it is the thickness you desire.

PROTEIN

Season chicken and shrimp (separately) with salt, pepper, and Cajun seasoning.

Refrigerate until a little later.

Add the sausage to the gumbo gravy (it cooks longer than the chicken and shrimp). Cook on medium for 1 hour.

Add chicken. Cook on medium for an additional hour.

Add shrimp. Cook on medium for an additional 30 minutes.

Serve over cooked rice.

ROUX

1–2 cups olive oil
3–4 cups flour

GUMBO GRAVY

1 gallon water

2 bunches green onions, chopped

1 large yellow onion, chopped

salt and pepper

red pepper flakes

"Slap Ya Momma" Cajun Seasoning

PROTEIN

4 boneless chicken breasts, cubed

4 boneless chicken legs, cubed

4 boneless chicken thighs, cubed

2 lbs medium shrimp, peeled and devined

salt and pepper

red pepper flakes

"Slap Ya Momma" Cajun Seasoning

6 beef sausage links cut into 1/2" pieces

Serving Tip: rice, prepared

SOUPS & SANDWICHES

113

Cheeseburger Soup

Prep Time: 30 min

Cook Time: 30 min

Yields: 6–8 servings

Cook the beef, seasoning with salt and pepper. Drain. Set aside.

In the same pan, use 1 tbsp butter to sauté onion until tender.

Add potatoes and broth to the beef, Boil until potatoes are tender.

In a separate pan, melt remaining butter and add flour. Cook until incorporated, making a roux.

Add roux to the beef/potato/broth mixture to thicken.

Stir in cream, cheese, and milk.

Continue to stir until the cheese melts.

Top with bacon and jalapeños.

- 1 lb ground beef
- 8 tbsp (1 stick) butter
- 1 yellow onion, diced
- 2–3 russet potatoes, peeled and diced
- 6 cups chicken broth
- 1/3 cup flour
- 1 cup cream
- 4 cups shredded Velveeta cheese
- 2 cups milk
- bacon, crumbled (optional)
- jalapeños, chopped (optional)

Makes a great appetizer. Our beautiful daughter, Wren, loves burgers and anything with cheese. If she's having soup, she'll pick this one every time.

JB & Jamie

JB & Jamie

JB has loved this since he was kid.
You have to serve it with bacon!

Monterey Jack Cheese Soup

Prep Time: 5 min   Cook Time: 30 min   Yields: 5 servings

Cook bacon. Set aside.

In a saucepan, combine broth, Ro-Tel, onion, and garlic. Bring to a boil.

Reduce heat, cover, and simmer 10 minutes until onions are tender.

Remove from heat.

In another saucepan, melt butter.

Stir in flour until smooth, adding salt and pepper to taste.

Gradually add 1 1/2 cups of the milk, bringing it to a boil but stirring often.

As it begins to thicken, reduce heat, and add cooked onion mixture.

Add remaining milk.

Add cheese. Cook over low heat until cheese is melted.

Crumble bacon and lightly place on top after scooping soup into serving bowls.

Serve while hot!

- 4 strips bacon
- 1 cup chicken broth
- 10 oz can Ro-Tel (diced tomatoes with green chilies)
- 1/2 cup onion, diced
- 1 garlic clove, minced
- 2 tbsp butter
- 2 tbsp flour
- salt
- pepper
- 3 cups whole milk
- 2 cups shredded Monterey Jack cheese

SOUPS & SANDWICHES

Chicken 'n' Dumplings

Prep Time: 30 min

Cook Time: 45 min

Yields: 8–10 servings

Boil water. Add chicken base.

Return to boil.

Add sautéed vegetables (carrots, onions, and celery), if desired.

Season water with salt, pepper, and Italian seasoning to taste.

Add deboned chicken to boiling water.

In a bowl, mix Bisquick and milk to make thick and fluffy dumplings.

Drop dumplings by the spoonful into the boiling water.

Cook about 15 minutes.

20 cups water

4 tbsp chicken base (makes the best stock)

sautéed carrots, onions, and celery (if desired)

salt

pepper

Italian seasoning

1 rotisserie chicken, deboned

5 cups Bisquick (don't judge)

1 1/2 cups milk

This was JB's favorite meal as a kid! JB's mom (Sadie and Wren called her "Gommy") made the best dumplings. He's had them all kinds of ways, but this is his favorite, and it will be yours too! It's a cheap meal, but it's so good. Gommy made them once a week.

JB & Jamie

SOUPS & SANDWICHES

JB & Jamie

This is the soup that JB's family would make to warm themselves up their cold house. The warm soup paired with the kick from the jalapeños give it just the heat you need to kick the chill!

Royers Jalapeño Cheese Soup

Prep Time: 30 min **Cook Time: 30 min** **Yields: 7–8 servings**

Melt butter in a skillet.

Add baking soda, flour, and cornstarch. Mix together until thick to make roux.

In a large stock pot, bring water, bouillon cubes, and jalapeños to a boil.

Add roux to boiling water. Stir until thickened and it begins to boil again.

Add milk. Mix completely.

Reduce heat to medium-low.

Add sliced cheese, one slice at a time, continuing to stir until melted.

Add onion, celery, and carrots.

Cover pot and turn off heat. Let sit until vegetables are tender.

- 4 tbsp butter
- 1 tsp baking soda
- 3/4 cup flour
- 6 tbsp cornstarch
- 6 cups water
- 16 chicken bouillon cubes, crushed
- 2 tbsp jalapeños, minced
- 6 cups milk
- 1 lb sliced American cheese
- 1 medium onion, chopped
- 1/2 cup celery, chopped
- 1/2 cup carrots, chopped

This soup is a staple at the Cafe. We've been serving it since the winter of 1987. This is a Royers Cafe menu fave, and it freezes well! It's just delicious. Eat it with rolls or grilled bread.

JB & Jamie

Hot Nashville Chicken Sandwich

 Prep Time: 15 min Cook Time: 10 min Yields: 4 servings

Prepare 2 bowls:

Bowl 1 (Wet): Combine buttermilk and 2 tbsp Royers Meat Seasoning Rub.

Bowl 2 (Dry): Combine flour and 1 tbsp Royers Meat Seasoning Rub.

Dip chicken breasts in buttermilk mixture (wet) and then roll in flour mixture (dry) to coat the breasts completely.

Fry chicken breasts in oil until completely cooked (about 4 minutes on each side or to 165°F).

Dip cooked chicken in Nashville Sauce and place on your favorite bun.

In a bowl, combine shredded cabbage with Royers Blue Cheese Dressing to make a simple blue cheese slaw.

Top the Nashville chicken with the blue cheese slaw and a handful of pickles.

NASHVILLE SAUCE

In separate pan, mix all Nashville Sauce ingredients on low heat until well mixed and fully melted.

2 1/2 cups buttermilk

3 tbsp Royers Meat Seasoning Rub (p. 258)

4 chicken breasts (boneless/skinless)

2 cups flour

vegetable oil (1 inch in skillet)

favorite buns (4)

1 bag cabbage, shredded

Royers Blue Cheese Dressing (p. 246)

jar of sliced pickles

NASHVILLE SAUCE

8 tbsp (1 stick) butter

1 tbsp cayenne

1 tbsp paprika

1 tbsp course pepper

1/2 cup Frank's RedHot

1 tbsp garlic, minced

1/2 cup brown sugar

Savannah Chicken Sandwich

 Prep Time: 15 min

 Cook Time: 8 min

 Yields: 4 servings

Prepare 2 bowls:

Bowl 1 (Wet): Combine buttermilk and 2 tbsp Royers Meat Seasoning Rub.

Bowl 2 (Dry): Combine flour and 1 tbsp Royers Meat Seasoning Rub.

Dip chicken breasts in buttermilk mixture (wet) and then roll in flour mixture (dry) to coat the breasts completely.

Fry chicken breasts in oil until completely cooked (about 4 minutes on each side or to 165°F).

Place cooked chicken on your favorite bun.

Top with goat cheese and a healthy pour of Frank's RedHot sweet chili sauce.

2 1/2 cups buttermilk

3 tbsp Royers Meat Seasoning Rub (p. 258)

4 chicken breasts (boneless/skinless)

2 cups flour

vegetable oil (1 inch in skillet)

favorite hamburger buns (4)

8 oz goat cheese

Frank's RedHot sweet chili sauce

Inspired by Savannah, Georgia, the creaminess of the goat cheese works extremely well with the sweet chili and the fried chicken.

JB & Jamie

Royers Grilled Pimento Cheese Sandwich

 Prep Time: 10 min   **Cook Time: 10 min**   **Yields: 4 servings**

Cook bacon (can leave in slices).

Top each side of bun/bread with a dollop of Bobbi's Pimento Cheese Dip and smooth out with a spatula.

Place 2 slices of bacon on one side.

Add any veggies you would like to make the sandwich more robust.

Place the two breads (with all of the yumminess in the middle) together.

Heat a skillet and grill each side until golden brown.

8 slices bacon

favorite bun/bread

Bobbi's Pimento Cheese Dip (p. 31)

Your choice of veggies (optional)

This is Jamie's favorite sandwich!

JB & Jamie

JB & Jamie

This is like a margherita pizza in sandwich form.
You can add chicken or shrimp for more protein.

Pesto Panini

Prep Time: 5 min   **Cook Time: 2–3 min**   **Yields: 2 servings**

Top panini bread starting with pesto. Add tomatoes, basil, and mozzarella.

Get your panini press hot, and brush with olive oil.

Place sandwich on press for 2–3 minutes. You can also grill in a cast iron skillet.

4 slices panini bread

1 jar of your favorite pesto

1 large tomato, sliced

few sprigs of basil

1/2 log fresh mozzarella, sliced

olive oil

If you want the fun ridges you can grab a cast iron that has them (Lodge sells one). Get one of those, and put a weight on top of the sandwich and your bread will have the perfect panini-type ridges.

JB & Jamie

JB & Jamie

Jamie grew up eating these all the time.
You can serve them as a panini or on a hoagie bun.

Italian Hero Panini

Prep Time: 5 min   **Cook Time: 2–3 min**   **Yields: 2 servings**

Layer panini bread with pizza sauce, jalapeños, pepperoni, ham, and provolone cheese.

Get your panini press hot, and brush with olive oil.

Place sandwich on press for 2–3 minutes. You can also grill in a cast iron skillet.

4 slices panini bread

1 jar pizza sauce

few slices pickled jalapeños

handful of sliced pepperoni

1 lb ham

1 package provolone cheese

olive oil

If you want the fun ridges you can grab a cast iron that has them (Lodge sells one). Get one of those, and put a weight on top of the sandwich and your bread will have the perfect panini-type ridges.

JB & Jamie

JB & Jamie

This sandwich has an incredible flavor profile with the creamy brie, salty turkey and sweet blueberries.

Turkey Blueberry Brie Panini

Prep Time: 5 min   Cook Time: 2–3 min   Yields: 2 servings

Put blueberries in a skillet with the sugar and jalapeños and cook down until it forms a thick sauce.

Cut off outer rind of brie and slice into 1/4" slices.

Top bread with blueberry mixture, turkey, and a couple slices of brie.

Place another slice of bread on top.

Get your panini press hot, and brush with olive oil.

Place sandwich on press for 2–3 minutes. You can also grill in a cast iron skillet.

8 oz blueberries

2 tbsp sugar

1 tbsp jalapeños, diced

1/2 wheel brie

1 lb leftover turkey

4 slices panini bread

olive oil

If you want the fun ridges you can grab a cast iron that has them (Lodge sells one). Get one of those, and put a weight on top of the sandwich and your bread will have the perfect panini-type ridges.

JB & Jamie

Thanksgiving Leftover Panini

Prep Time: 5 min   Cook Time: 2–3 min   Yields: 2 servings

Top bread with turkey, dressing, and cranberry sauce.

Get your panini press hot, and brush with olive oil.

Place sandwich on press for 2–3 minutes. You can also grill in a cast iron skillet.

4 slices panini bread

1 lb leftover turkey

2 scoops leftover turkey dressing

1 can cranberry sauce

olive oil

If you want the fun ridges you can grab a cast iron that has them (Lodge sells one). Get one of those, and put a weight on top of the sandwich and your bread will have the perfect panini-type ridges.

— JB & Jamie —

Cafe Classic Burger

 Prep Time: 5 min

 Cook Time: 10 min

 Yields: 2 servings

Make 2 8-oz patties.

Cook to desired temperature, seasoning both sides with Royers Grilling Seasoning.

Top with Royers Dill Butter.

Grill.

Butter buns and toast in skillet.

Place one patty on each bun and add your favorite toppings.

1 lb hamburger meat

Royers Grilling Seasoning (p. 259)

Royers Dill Butter (p. 256)

2 challah buns (or your favorite hamburger bun)

1 tbsp butter

your favorite burger toppings

Just a good old grass-fed beef burger!

JB & Jamie

Southern Fried Burger

Prep Time: 15 min   **Cook Time: 15 min**   **Yields: 2 servings**

Make 2 8-oz Cafe Classic Burger patties.

Cook to desired temperature, seasoning both sides with Royers Grilling Seasoning.

Top with Royers Dill Butter.

Grill.

Butter buns,and toast in skillet.

Place one patty on each bun.

Add 1/2 cup Bobbi's Pimento Cheese Dip and 3 slices of Tiny Cajun's Fried Green Tomatoes to each patty.

Add any of your other favorite toppings.

2 Cafe Classic Burgers (p. 137)

Royers Grilling Seasoning (p.259)

Royers Dill Butter (p. 256)

2 buns of your choice

1 cup Bobbi's Pimento Cheese Dip (p. 31)

6 Tiny Cajun's Fried Green Tomatoes (p. 33)

Another great way to eat a burger! Get ready to make your kitchen a little messy with this burger, and then fill some tummies! JB calls this a heart attack on a bun. It's a Southern twist to a classic burger.

JB & Jamie

SOUPS & SANDWICHES

Wren's Patty Melt

Prep Time: 15 min

Cook Time: 15 min

Yields: 2 servings

Make 4 4-oz patties.

Cook, seasoning both sides with Royers Grilling Seasoning.

Top with a little Royers Dill Butter.

Cook to desired temperature.

Butter Texas toast and toast in skillet.

Grill sliced onion in skillet.

Place one patty on bread and top with grilled onions.

Place second patty on top and add a dollop of Wren sauce.

1 lb hamburger meat

Royers Grilling Seasoning (p. 259)

Royers Dill Butter (p. 256)

butter

4 slices Texas toast

1 red onion, sliced

Wren Sauce (p. 253)

Wren loves In-N-Out Burger, especially the onion-style sauce. Jamie and Wren enjoyed working together in the kitchen to create their own perfect onion blend for this sauce. They wanted to create a sauce that would compliment the patty and grilled onions.

JB & Jamie

JB & Jamie

The perfect touch is a perfect bun! We love using Shelia
Partin's Jalapeño & Cheese Sourdough Buns!

(www.sbakery.com)

Royers Grilled Shrimp BLT

Prep Time: 20 min

Cook Time: 15 min

Yields: 4 servings

Heat a thin layer of Royers Dill Butter in a medium-sized cast iron skillet.

Add shrimp to skillet and season with Royers Grilling Seasoning.

When the shrimp are cooked, lay them on a paper towel to dry.

Cook bacon in skillet until slices are nice and crispy. Then lay bacon on paper towel to dry.

Put the sandwich together.

First, spread Royers Smokin' Mesquite Mustard on both sides of the bun.

Lay 3–4 rings of onion, then lettuce, and then tomato slices on half of bun.

Add shrimp and bacon slices, and close sandwich.

Cut in half and put a toothpick in each half to help hold it together!

Royers Dill Butter (p. 256)

1 lb Gulf shrimp

Royers Grilling Seasoning (p. 259)

12 thick bacon slices

Royers Smokin' Mesquite Mustard (mail order)

4 Shelia Partin's Jalapeño & Cheese Sourdough Buns

1 medium red onion, peeled and sliced

4 green leaf lettuce leaves

2 medium tomatoes, sliced

Served on a Shelia Partin's Jalapeño & Cheese Bun with Royers Smokin' Mesquite Mustard, Gulf shrimp, and thick bacon—OMG! This grilled shrimp BLT is one of the most ordered items at the Cafe.

JB & Jamie

MEATS

Meat is the star of the whole meal. It's what people are most interested in at our Cooking Classes. Your appetizers, sides, and drinks are all paired around it, as we showcase at every Wine Dinner. Achieving that perfect harmony is all about the seasoning and the timing, getting that juicy depth of flavor from the front of your mouth to the back of your throat and all the way down.

Have a meat thermometer on hand so you don't undercook or overcook it, and remember to let the meat rest. It's always better to undercook. You can't uncook a dried-out piece of meat, but you can always cook it longer. When I was growing up, everyone said, "You have to cook pork to 165°." If you cook pork to 165°, you'll get the most overcooked, dried-out piece of meat you've ever had. Pull it off the heat early, and let it rest before you cut into it. Letting the meat—pork, chicken, or beef—rest off the heat allows it to keep on cooking while sealing those juices inside without overcooking. If you cut it too early, the juices run and dry out the meat.

While you want to buy quality meat with great marbling, how you cook it will make all the difference. One time we treated Sadie and Wren to a nice meal out. Wren ordered an 8-ounce filet of wagyu—the most expensive cut on the market. It came out great, but when the waiter asked how her steak was, she didn't think twice before responding. "Not as good as my mom and dad's," she said casually.

Jamie and I could have crawled under the table.

It was a heck of a piece of meat, but steaks are all about how you cook them. You don't have to buy wagyu filet to make a great steak. You add a little love, pack the right seasoning on there, cook it just right, and you're good.

JB & Jamie

Super easy dinner your whole family will love.
Makes great leftovers!

Slow Cooker Pot Roast

Prep Time: 30 min

Cook Time: 8–10 hours

Yields: 6–8 servings

Place roast in crock-pot.

Add beef bone broth and all seasonings.

Place pepperoncinis, ghee, mushrooms, onions, and carrots around roast.

Cook on low 8–10 hours.

Serve over Garlic Mashed Potatoes.

3 lb chuck roast

1 cup beef bone broth

1 tbsp coco aminos

3–6 cloves garlic (depends on how much you like garlic)

1 tbsp dried parsley

1 tsp dried chives

1 tsp dill

2 tsp garlic powder

1 tsp onion powder

1 tbsp onion flakes

1 tsp black pepper

1 tsp pink salt

8–10 pepperoncinis

3 tbsp ghee (optional)

8 oz sliced mushrooms

1 yellow onion, sliced

3–4 carrots, chopped

Serving Tip: Garlic Mashed Potatoes (p. 85)

MEATS

Braised Short Ribs

Prep Time: 30 min   Cook Time: 3 hours   Yields: 8 servings

Instructions	Ingredients
In a bowl, mix together flour, salt, pepper, and Tony's Seasoning to make a seasoned flour mixture.	1 cup flour
	1 tsp salt
	1 tsp pepper
Crust short ribs with Grilling Seasoning and then roll in seasoned flour mixture.	1 tsp Tony Chachere's Creole Seasoning
Cook bacon in Dutch oven or cast iron for the grease. Remove bacon and set aside.	8 bone-in beef short ribs
	1/2 cup Royers Grilling Seasoning (p. 259)
Sear each side of the short ribs in bacon grease and set aside.	8 slices bacon
Add red wine to deglaze pot. Let this cook for a few minutes.	2 cups red wine
	2 cups beef broth
Add beef broth, onion, mushrooms, and rosemary. Cook 3 - 5 minutes.	1 medium yellow onion, chopped
Add beef ribs back to the pot.	1 package mushrooms, sliced
Bake at 350°F for 2 1/2–3 hours or until meat is falling off the bone.	2 sprigs rosemary
Great on top of Garlic Mashed Potatoes.	Serving Tip: Garlic Mashed Potatoes (p. 85)

This new Cafe special is just as good as a steak! If you have any left over the next day, it makes a killer beef sandwich.

JB & Jamie

JB & Jamie

This Beef Wellington is a staple for our Christmas Cooking Class—and a single man's dream. You can make yourself look really good when you cook this very simple dish. Preparation is key. Make sure you have the duxelles (mushroom paste) ready ahead of time.

Royers Beef Wellington

 Prep Time: 45 min   **Cook Time: 45 min**   **Yields: 4 servings**

Preheat oven to 425°F.

In a pan, add olive oil, mushrooms, salt, and pepper.

Cook down mushrooms over medium heat until the moisture is cooked out (this will take some time, roughly 15–20 minutes).

Add garlic and shallot to the mixture and continue to cook down.

Cool down the mixture in the fridge as you begin to assemble the Wellington.

Roll out the puff pastry to fit (wrap) the filets.

Rub on a small amount of mustard across the top of each puff pastry.

Lay prosciutto across each puff pastry.

Spread a layer of mushroom paste (mixture) on top of each prosciutto layer.

Place each filet in the center of its own puff pastry.

Fold the puff pastry up and over the filet to wrap like a small gift.

Add a touch of butter to the top of the pastry dough.

Bake until golden brown.

Serve with Garlic Mashed Potatoes.

1/4 cup olive oil

8 oz button mushrooms, chopped

1/2 tsp salt

1/2 tsp pepper

2 garlic cloves, finely chopped

1 shallot, finely chopped

puff pastry dough*

4 8-oz filets

1 tbsp mustard

4 pieces prosciutto

Royers Grilling Seasoning (p. 259)

Serving Tip: Garlic Mashed Potatoes (p. 85)

* Find puff pastries in the freezer section of your grocery store.

MEATS

Grandma's Roasted Turkey

Prep Time: 30 min   **Cook Time: 3 hours**   **Yields: 14–16 servings**

Place turkey in metal pan.

Season liberally with olive oil and then garlic powder, Tony Chachere's Creole Seasoning, salt, pepper, and poultry seasoning.

Make sure you have chicken stock in the bottom of the pan to add to the turkey later on.

Wrap the turkey tightly in foil and put in the oven at 325°F.

Cook for the first hour unopened and then begin to baste the turkey with stock every half hour.

Wait for the turkey to reach 165°F internal temperature in the thickest part, but don't overcook it!

Take the foil off as you approach 165°F to get it golden brown and then let it rest!

1 turkey, 14–16 pounds

(Figure a pound per person, including bones. It might seem like a lot of weight, but when you factor in the bones, it's really not a lot.)

1 cup olive oil

garlic powder

Tony Chachere's Creole Seasoning

salt

pepper

poultry seasoning

chicken stock

JB's grandmother was an excellent cook and we enjoy celebrating Thanksgiving every year by using her recipe for the customers at the Cafe. We're pretty big on Thanksgiving dinner, and this (along with Coach's Green Beans) is simple and delicious.

— JB & Jamie —

Meatloaf

Prep Time: 10 min   Cook Time: 1.5 hours   Yields: 4 servings

Preheat oven to 350°F.

Put hamburger meat in a bowl.

Season with salt, pepper, and Tony Chachere's Creole Seasoning. Mix together.

Add tomato sauce, egg, Ritz crackers, and onion. Mix together.

Put in a loaf pan or a 9" x 9" pan and top with tomato sauce with Italian herbs.

Cover with foil and bake 1 hour.

Remove foil after an hour.

Bake for an additional 30 minutes uncovered or until top is cooked and meatloaf is shrinking away from the sides.

Serve with your favorite side.

1 lb hamburger meat

salt

pepper

Tony Chachere's Creole Seasoning

1 can tomato sauce

1 egg

1 tube Ritz crackers, crushed

1 yellow onion, diced

1 can tomato sauce with Italian herbs

Jamie makes the best meatloaf. The next day, it's perfect for a sandwich. Grab your favorite bread, toast it up, and put a slice of meatloaf on it.

Enjoy the yummy sandwich.

JB & Jamie

MEATS

Royers Sunday Fried Chicken

 Prep Time: 10 min   **Cook Time:** 30 min   **Yields:** 6–8 servings

Mix together buttermilk, 1/4 cup Royers Meat Seasoning Rub, and garlic powder.

Place chicken pieces in buttermilk mixture to marinate. Refrigerate 24 hours.

In a bowl, mix together flour and 1/4 cup meat seasoning Rub.

Heat grease in fryer to approx. 300°F.

Remove chicken from the buttermilk mixture and immediately roll each piece of chicken separately in flour, coating completely.

Carefully place chicken into the fryer. We suggest frying breasts and thighs together approx. 18 minutes.

Fry legs and wings together approx. 10 minutes.

8 cups buttermilk

1/2 cup Royers Meat Seasoning Rub (p. 258)

1/4 cup Spice Islands garlic powder (not garlic salt!)

8 cups flour

2 whole chickens, cut into parts

frying grease

Chicken is *delish* served cold the next day! Sunday Fried Chicken is marinated 24 hours in garlic, spices, buttermilk, and Royers Meat Seasoning Rub. True to its name, it's served only on Sundays, although the leftovers go in our Buffalo Chicken Salad. (Oh, and you can make it any day of the week!)

JB & Jamie

MEATS

Todd's Grilled Pork Tenderloin

 Prep Time: 5 min   **Cook Time: 15–20 min**   **Yields: 3–4 servings**

Coat the tenderloin with Royers Grilling Seasoning.

Heat 3 tbsp of Royers Dill Butter in a cast iron skillet.

Place tenderloin in the heated skillet.

Once tenderloin is halfway done, cut center to butterfly and baste with remaining Royers Dill Butter.

Cook until inside is pink and tender. Don't overcook!

Plate on serving dish.

Top with Royers Peach 'N' Pepper Glaze.

1 lb pork tenderloin

Royers Grilling Seasoning (p. 259)

6 tbsp Royers Dill Butter (p. 256)

6 tbsp Royers Peach 'N' Pepper Glaze (p. 251)

Another Cafe staple, a popular catering order, and JB's brother Todd's favorite pork dish.

— JB & Jamie —

MEATS

Royers Great Steak

Prep Time: 2 min   **Cook Time:** 20–25 min   **Yields:** 2 servings

Preheat cast iron skillet.

Heavily crust all sides of filets with Royers Grilling Seasoning.

Place filets on a cast iron skillet with Royers Dill Butter. Turn while cooking so all sides are evenly crusted.

Cook to preferred temperature.

While steaks are cooking, grill onions on the same cast iron skillet. (Be sure to grill the onions using the juice from the steak.)

Top steak with grilled onions.

2 10-oz center-cut filets

Royers Grilling Seasoning (p. 259)

2 tbsp Royers Dill Butter (p. 256)

1 red onion, sliced

This is the Cafe's number-one seller. It's what people come to the Cafe for. We cook it at every Wine Dinner and Cooking Class because it's hands down the Rolls Royce of all filets!

JB & Jamie

MEATS

Lil' Miss Red's Rack of Lamb

Prep Time: 5 min   **Cook Time: 20 min**   **Yields: 2 servings**

Preheat cast iron skillet.

Crust both sides of rack of lamb with Royers Grilling Seasoning.

Cut each rib 3/4 of the way through. (The rack will spread open.)

Melt a small amount of Royers Dill Butter in skillet. Place rack cut side up. Flip and cook evenly to preferred temperature.

When done, serve with Lemon Garlic Basil Sauce.

1 lb rack of lamb

Royers Grilling Seasoning (p. 259)

1/2 cup Royers Dill Butter (p. 256)

1/2 cup Lemon Garlic Basil Sauce (p. 254)

We named this recipe after a little seven-year-old girl who used to come to the Cafe with her parents. All she'd order was the $40 rack of lamb. This recipe will make you a lamb fan. It's been a Cafe favorite for a long time. It's great for family gatherings as an entrée or cut into lamb lollipops for appetizers.

JB & Jamie

MEATS

163

Mom's Chicken Fried Steak

Prep Time: 10 min   Cook Time: 14 min   Yields: 4 servings

Heat vegetable oil in a large cast iron skillet.

Prepare 2 bowls:

Bowl 1 (Dry): Combine flour, salt, pepper, and Tonys seasoning.

Bowl 2 (Wet): Combine Meat Seasoning and eggs. Mix well.

Dip/roll steaks into flour mixture (dry), then egg mixture (wet), then flour mixture (dry). Make sure you coat both sides thoroughly.

Place steaks in heated skillet.

Pan fry the steaks until the crust is golden brown, turning to cook both sides. (The less turning you do, the better chance the breading will not become dislodged in the process.)

Be sure to keep enough oil in the skillet so the steak is cooked from the hot oil and not from the hot skillet.

To serve, smother the steaks with Mae Dell's Gravy.

1 cup vegetable oil

2 tsp Royers Meat Seasoning Rub (p. 258)

6 eggs

4 5-oz or 6-oz round steaks*
(1 per person)
*meat should be tenderized twice

4 cups flour

1 tbsp salt

1 tbsp pepper

1 tbsp Tony Chachere's Creole Seasoning

Mae Dell's Gravy (p.257)

This is Jamie's mama's recipe.
Pan fried is the way to go on this one.

JB & Jamie

MEATS

165

Karen's Lemon Chicken

Prep Time: 10 min   Cook Time: 12 min   Yields: 8 servings

Dip chicken in lemon juice and roll in 1 cup grated Parmesan cheese.

Roll in flour.

Fry chicken in vegetable oil on medium heat.

Don't overcook it!

After cooked, sprinkle each piece with lemon juice, remaining grated Parmesan cheese and top with parsley.

8 skinless, boneless chicken breasts

1 cup lemon juice

1 1/4 cups grated Parmesan cheese

2 cups flour

vegetable oil

parsley (optional)

This was one of the first dishes we served at the Cafe, and now it's a tribute to JB's mom, Karen—the Queen Mother of the Royer family—who came up with the recipe.

JB & Jamie

JB & Jamie

How do you make a "Great Steak" even better?!

By serving it like we do here at the Cafe. We place it up on a couple scoops of Royers Mashed Potato Casserole and top it with our secret sauce (Awesome Sauce)!

Royers Steak Special

Prep Time: 15 min **Cook Time: 20 min** **Yields: 2 servings**

Preheat cast iron skillet.

Heavily crust all sides of filets with Royers Grilling Seasoning.

Place filets on a cast iron skillet with Royers Dill Butter. Turn while cooking so all sides are evenly crusted.

Cook to preferred temperature.

We suggest plating the steak on a heaping serving of Mashed Potato Casserole.

Top with Royers Awesome Steak Sauce.

Awesome Steak Sauce

Heat Royers Dill Butter in skillet with rosemary, red onion, and mushrooms. Cook until onions are translucent.

Add red wine and Bud's Marination. Let wine cook out, constantly stirring for about 2 minutes.

Add heavy whipping cream. Lower heat to low and let sauce thicken.

Use as a topping for steak filets or as a dip for rolls.

2 10-oz center-cut filets

Royers Grilling Seasoning (p. 259)

2 tbsp Royers Dill Butter (p. 256)

Royers Awesome Steak Sauce

Serving Tip: Royers Mashed Potato Casserole (p. 101)

Awesome Sauce

1/4 cup Royers Dill Butter (p. 256)

2 shakes rosemary

1 red onion, diced

8 oz portabella mushrooms, sliced

1 cup red wine

1/4 cup Bud's Marination (p. 257)

1 cup heavy whipping cream

MEATS

SEAFOODS

Seafood has become more of a Southern comfort food—especially fried catfish and shrimp 'n' grits. Those are great, but seafood doesn't have to be fried to be good. Season it well, and then cook it in a skillet, in the oven, or on the grill. Use our Royers Dill Butter (p. 256), a little seasoning, a little sauce, and it's delicious.

The key to a good seafood dish is the freshness and flavor of the ingredients. We bring in Gulf snapper and Gulf shrimp and pack them with flavor. There's nothing worse than taking a bite of fish and thinking, "That's fishy." Seafood is a lot like chicken; you often have to create flavor while not overcooking it. Otherwise, it becomes rubbery real quick.

A lot of people think they don't like fish, but many times they've just had poorly cooked fish or only one kind of fish. When you are first testing out your kitchen skill on fish (and your personal taste preferences) make sure you test a selection of fish —salmon, snapper, flounder, halibut—and experiment until you find what you like. Some people like a firmer fish such as halibut instead of a watery, flaky fish such as cod. Cooking with different seasonings and sauces on the fish also gives a variety and range to these dishes.

A key to remember with seafood is that you are not limited to fish. Shrimp! Crab! Mussels! Calamari! There are so many options and what it really all comes down to is how you prepare it and what you pair it with. Pairing your seafood with a fun side opens you up to so many possibilities. A simple fish recipe paired with cheese grits will taste dramatically different served over a bed of rice or alongside twice baked potatoes.

The cooking world is your oyster! Speaking of oysters - try them with the Royers Horseradish Dressing (a surprisingly yummy combination)!

Blackened Snapper with Pontchartrain

Prep Time: 10 min

Cook Time: 30 min

Yields: 4 servings

Reduce heavy whipping cream in a pot on the stove on low heat, letting the liquid cook down until about half is remaining in the pot (approx. 30 minutes). Be sure to stir, but do not scrape the bottom of the pan during the reduction.

Add cold butter and seasoning.

Once butter is incorporated, add cooked crab and shrimp.

Bring sauce to a slow boil, stirring occasionally.

Coat snapper with blackening seasoning and cook in a pan about 2–3 minutes per side, until fish is cooled and flaky.

Serve fish on a plate of wild rice and top with sauce.

- 2 cups heavy whipping cream
- 8 tbsp (1 stick) butter, cold
- blackening seasoning (enough to coat fish + 2 tbsp)
- 1/4 lb cooked crab meat
- 1/4 lb cooked shrimp
- 4 8-oz snapper filets

Serving Tip: wild rice, prepared

This Pontchartrain sauce includes fresh crab and shrimp. Put it over a blackened snapper, and it'll coat your mouth all the way down to your stomach! A great topper to almost any fish. It's just phenomenal.

JB & Jamie

SEAFOODS

Cyndi's Coconut Shrimp

Prep Time: 20 min

Cook Time: 10 min

Yields: 3–4 servings

Rinse shrimp in cold water and pat dry.

Prepare 3 bowls:

Bowl 1: Stir together flour, garlic powder, and salt.

Bowl 2: Beat eggs.

Bowl 3: Mix together Panko and coconut flakes.

Roll shrimp in flour mixture (bowl 1), dip in egg (bowl 2), and then dip in Panko mixture (bowl 3) . Use your hands to press the coconut crumb mixture onto your shrimp.

Place a large pan over medium heat add enough oil to generously cover the bottom.

Once the oil is hot, sauté shrimp for 2 minutes per side until golden brown.

1 lb large shrimp, peeled and deveined

1/4 cup all purpose flour

1/2 tsp garlic powder

1/2 tsp salt

2 large eggs, beaten

1/2 cup Panko breadcrumbs

1 1/2 cups sweetened, shredded coconut

vegetable oil

This is a perfect summer dish.
Try topping it with mango salsa.

JB & Jamie

Jumbo Lump Crab Cakes

 Prep Time: 10 min   **Cook Time:** 5 min   **Yields:** 3 servings

In a large bowl, mix together all ingredients.

Form 4 rather large cakes or 8 small cakes if you're making an appetizer.

Place on baking sheet, and refrigerate at least 30 minutes to allow them to set up.

Once you're ready to cook, heat your frying oil of choice in a pan on the stove.

When oil is hot, drop the cakes in the pan and cook 1–2 minutes on each side until golden brown.

For a little zing, top them with Royers Creamy Cajun Sauce.

1 lb crab meat (sold at most seafood counters)

1 cup saltines, crushed

1 tbsp Dijon mustard

1 tbsp Worcestershire sauce

1/2 cup mayonnaise

dash of Louisiana hot sauce (unless you're me and your dash is like 8–10 dashes)

pepper

Tony Chachere's Creole Seasoning

Frying oil of choice

Royers Creamy Cajun Sauce (p. 247)

(optional)

We modeled these after Maryland crab cakes, so they aren't breaded—just mixed with mayonnaise, crab, and then grilled. They're a hit in our Cooking Classes.

JB & Jamie

Corey's Shrimp 'N' Grits

 Prep Time: 30 min   **Cook Time: 30 min**   **Yields: 10–12 servings**

Boil water.	9 cups water
Add jalapeños, garlic, paprika, cayenne, salt, and butter.	4 tbsp jalapeños, chopped
Add grits to boiling mixture and whisk until all water is absorbed.	4 tbsp garlic, minced
Turn off burner and cover pan for 5 minutes.	1 tsp paprika
Add eggs and stir so they do not scramble.	1 tsp cayenne
Add cream cheese. Mix.	2 tbsp salt
Add pepper jack cheese, American cheese, heavy whipping cream and water (up to 4 additional cups when you need more liquid).	16 tbsp (2 sticks) butter
Turn heat down to low.	24 oz quick grits
Serve grits in a bowl with grilled shrimp stacked on top.	1 cup eggs

Ingredients (right column continued):

- 9 cups water
- 4 tbsp jalapeños, chopped
- 4 tbsp garlic, minced
- 1 tsp paprika
- 1 tsp cayenne
- 2 tbsp salt
- 16 tbsp (2 sticks) butter
- 24 oz quick grits
- 1 cup eggs
- 8 oz cream cheese
- 2 1/4 lbs pepper jack cheese
- 1 1/2 lb American cheese
- 4 cups water
- 1 qt heavy whipping cream

GRILLED SHRIMP

In a medium-sized cast iron skillet, heat a thin layer of Royers Dill Butter.

Add shrimp to skillet and season with Royers Grilling Seasoning.

When the shrimp are cooked, lay them on a paper towel to dry.

GRILLED SHRIMP

Royers Dill Butter (p. 256)

4 lb shrimp

Royers Grilling Seasoning (p. 259)

SEAFOODS

179

Fresh Cod with Citrus Butter

Prep Time: 10 min

Cook Time: 10 min

Yields: 2 servings

olive oil

2 8-oz pieces of fresh cod

course ground pepper

Royers Grilling Seasoning (p. 259)

Coat pan with olive oil and place on burner to heat up the oil.

Place fish in pan with hot oil.

Season with Royers Grilling Seasoning.

Cook on each side about 3 minutes.

Top with Citrus Butter.

CITRUS BUTTER

2 tbsp butter, melted

1 tsp minced garlic

1 orange
- juice from entire orange
- zest from 1/2 orange

1 lemon
- juice from entire lemon
- zest from 1/2 lemon

salt

pepper

CITRUS BUTTER

In a bowl, mix butter, garlic, orange juice, orange zest, lemon juice, and lemon zest.

Add salt and pepper to taste.

You'll want to drink this citrus butter! This recipe works with any white fish, so pick your favorite fish and enjoy!

JB & Jamie

Mike's Fish Tacos

Prep Time: 60 min

Cook Time: 15 min

Yields: 4 servings

Dice red onion and put in sealed container with red wine vinegar.

Let marinate in the refrigerator for at least 1 hour (best if left overnight).

Heat oil in skillet.

Season fish with Royers Grilling Seasoning and Royers Dill Butter and cook fish for 3 minutes on each side until fully cooked.

Heat tortillas until soft in microwave or on a dry skillet.

Put a drizzle of Royers Cilantro Ranch Dressing on tortillas.

Place fish into prepared tortillas.

In a bowl, toss cabbage with Royers Creamy Cajun Sauce for a delicious quick Cajun slaw.

Top with marinated red onions.

---

1 red onion

1 cup red wine vinegar

olive oil

4 white fish filets

Royers Grilling Seasoning (p. 259)

Royers Dill Butter (p. 256)

corn tortillas

Royers Cilantro Ranch Dressing (p. 249)

cabbage, chopped

Royers Creamy Cajun Sauce (p. 247)

You can try different fish or even shrimp—grilled, blackened, or fried.

JB & Jamie

SEAFOODS

Micah's Salmon or Snapper

 Prep Time: 10 min   Cook Time: 10 min   Yields: 4 servings

Melt a small amount of Royers Dill Butter on a cast iron skillet.

Place fish on grill, skin side down.

Sprinkle fish with Royers Grilling Seasoning and add more Royers Dill Butter.

When edges of fish are opaque in color, flip.

Remove skin and season with more Royers Grilling Seasoning and Royers Dill Butter.

Remove fish from grill and place on individual plates.

Top with Micah's Sauce and garnish with lemon wedge.

2 cups Royers Dill Butter (p. 256)

1 1/2 lbs salmon (or snapper)

Royers Grilling Seasoning (p. 259)

Micah's Sauce (p. 251)

1 lemon, cut in wedges

This is a Royers Cafe menu fave! Funny story—the first three or four times our best friends had us over, they made salmon. After the third time, when we were driving home, Jamie said, "Look, I've got to tell them because I cannot force myself to eat this again." We joke about it now, but the great thing about this recipe is that if salmon ain't your thing, you can sub snapper, which is less "fishy."

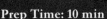 JB & Jamie

SEAFOODS

PASTAS

Here's the truth: we've never made fresh pasta noodles. We know we could if we wanted to. Anyone can read a recipe and learn that particular skill. But the secret to our amazing pastas isn't the pasta itself; it's all about the sauces. They're rich, but they're good because they go beyond the basic tomato sauce.

For a show-stopping sauce, use fresh ingredients—fresh tomatoes, vegetables, and herbs. Anybody can open a can of marinara, boil noodles, and throw cheese on top. You can have confidence in bringing your sauce to the next level with superior ingredients you can find in your local grocery store or your own garden. Add red wine, heavy cream, and our Royers Dill Butter (p. 256), and top it with shaved Parmesan cheese. You will elevate the dish by increasing and improving the flavor of those basic ingredients.

One of the best things about a pasta dish is that you can split the dish if your audience will have different taste preferences. If you know that there are kids coming over with the group you are hosting and they are picky eaters, you can make multiple sauces to enjoy over the same pasta. This allows you to keep it simple for the kids while you dazzle it up for the adults. Enjoy experimenting with adding in different types of heat (spices and peppers)!

The fun thing about the recipes in this section is that they're geographically from all over the place—We took the best flavors from all over the world to include in our pasta dishes and they are consistently praised by our loyal Cafe patrons, both for the amazing taste and the beautiful colors of the ingredients on the plate.

Audrey's Yo Face Pasta

 Prep Time: 10 min   **Cook Time: 25 min**   **Yields: 4 servings**

Combine Royers Dill Butter, garlic, onion, rosemary, and cayenne. Sauté until onions are translucent.

Once onions are cooked, add wine to pan and cook until the alcohol cooks out.

Add heavy whipping cream and bring to a boil.

Add shredded Parmesan cheese and stir constantly so cheese doesn't burn.

On the grill, cook fish and shrimp with more Royers Dill Butter and Royers Grilling Seasoning.

Prepare noodles, then strain.

Place cooked noodles in bowl and toss with grated Parmesan cheese.

Place fish and shrimp on top of the noodles.

Top with sauce.

Garnish with Parmesan cheese and parsley.

---

1 cup Royers Dill Butter (p. 256)

4 tbsp garlic, chopped

1 red onion, chopped

2 sprigs rosemary

1/2 tsp cayenne

1/4-1/2 cup red wine (something you want a glass of later)

4 cups heavy whipping cream

8 oz Parmesan cheese, shredded

2 lbs light white fish

1 lb Gulf shrimp

Royers Grilling Seasoning (p. 259)

1 lb of your favorite noodles

1/2 cup Parmesan cheese, grated

parsley (optional)

It's so good you'll want to stuff your face with it!

JB & Jamie

Creamy Rosemary Alfredo

Prep Time: 10 min   Cook Time: 15 min   Yields: 4 servings

Melt butter in a pot.

Add rosemary and minced garlic.

Add heavy whipping cream and bring to a boil.

Start adding shredded Parmesan cheese, stirring or whisking constantly so you don't burn the cheese.

Let simmer on low to thicken.

Prepare noodles, then strain.

Add noodles to the pot with the sauce.

After plating, garnish with grated Parmesan cheese and parsley.

8 tbsp (1 stick) butter

1 sprig rosemary

1 tbsp minced garlic (more if you love garlic)

2–3 cups heavy whipping cream

8 oz Parmesan cheese, shredded

1 lb of your favorite noodles

1/2 cup Parmesan cheese, grated

parsley (optional)

This one is popular with kids and picky eaters.

JB & Jamie

PASTAS

Juicy Pasta

 Prep Time: 15 min   Cook Time: 15 min   Yields: 4 servings

Instructions	Ingredients
Melt butter in skillet.	**8 tbsp (1 stick) butter**
Add cayenne, paprika, red pepper flakes, and garlic.	**1/2 tsp cayenne**
	1/2 tsp paprika
Add heavy whipping cream (make sure to add this last).	**1/2 tsp red pepper flakes**
Bring to a low simmer.	**1 tbsp garlic, chopped**
Cook your choice of protein in a separate pan.	**1/2 cup heavy whipping cream**
Add protein to pasta sauce, and keep on low simmer.	**Your choice of protein*** *1 lb shrimp, *1 package cooked sausage, or * 1/2 of each!
While sauce is cooking, prepare noodles.	
Strain noodles and toss with Parmesan cheese.	**1 lb of your favorite noodles**
Pour pasta sauce over noodles and top with Parmesan cheese.	**1/2 cup Parmesan cheese, grated**
Garnish with parsley.	**parsley (optional)**

We like a spicy sauce, and this one is a killer!
Spicy but oh so yummy!

— JB & Jamie —

PASTAS

Awesome Pasta

Prep Time: 15 min

Cook Time: 20 min

Yields: 4 servings

Sauté shrimp in Royers Dill Butter.

Add bell peppers, squash, carrots, mushrooms, and onions, Simmer in Royers Dill Butter.

Heat thoroughly until vegetables are tender.

Add Seasoned Salt and heavy whipping cream.

Bring to a full boil.

While sauce is cooking, prepare noodles.

Strain noodles and toss with Parmesan cheese.

Serve mixture over prepared noodles.

Garnish with Parmesan cheese and parsley.

2 lbs shrimp

1 cup Royers Dill Butter (p. 256)

2 green bell peppers, chunked

2–3 squash, chunked

2 carrots, sliced

1 portabella mushroom, sliced

1 red onion, sliced

2 tsp Seasoned Salt

1 1/2 cups heavy whipping cream

1 lb of your favorite noodles

1/2 cup Parmesan cheese, grated

parsley (optional)

A Royers Cafe menu fave! This was JB's mom's favorite pasta. You can substitute chicken for shrimp.

JB & Jamie

JB & Jamie

Note: If sauce tastes too much like wine, add more Seasoned Salt.
If sauce is too salty, add more wine.

Micah's Shrimp Garlic Pasta

Prep Time: 15 min

Cook Time: 20 min

Yields: 4 servings

In a large skillet, combine olive oil, shrimp, garlic, and red pepper.

Cook until the shrimp are half done.

Add tomatoes, basil, lemon, and Seasoned Salt.

Continue to cook until tomatoes are slightly soft.

Add white wine, bring to a boil, and then simmer.

While sauce is cooking, prepare noodles.

Strain noodles and toss with Parmesan cheese.

Top with shrimp mixture and sprinkle with additional Parmesan cheese.

Garnish with parsley.

1/4 cup olive oil

2 lbs shrimp

4 tbsp garlic, minced

1 tsp crushed red pepper

10 cherry tomatoes, halved

3/4 cup fresh basil, chopped

1/2 lemon, squeezed

2 tsp Seasoned Salt

2 cups Chardonnay

1 lb of your favorite noodles

1/2 cups Parmesan cheese, grated

parsley (optional)

This is the favorite dish of JB's brother Micah—and the Cafe's most ordered pasta!

JB & Jamie

PASTAS

Angus Pasta

Prep Time: 15 min **Cook Time: 20 min** **Yields: 4 servings**

Cook beef tenderloin on cast iron skillet to desired temperature.

In skillet, combine Royers Dill Butter, tomatoes, mushrooms, and green onions. Cook until tender.

Add red wine and Bud's Marination. Continue to cook on medium heat until alcohol cooks out.

Add heavy whipping cream and bring to a full boil.

Add cooked beef tenderloin.

While sauce is cooking, prepare noodles. Strain and toss with Parmesan cheese.

Serve mixture over pasta.

Garnish with Parmesan cheese and parsley.

1-1/4 lbs beef tenderloin chunks

1 cups Royers Dill Butter (p. 256)

10 cherry tomatoes, halved

2 portabella mushrooms, sliced

1 cup green onions, chopped

1/2 cup red wine

1/8 cup Bud's Marination (p. 257)

1 1/2 cup heavy whipping cream

1 lb of your favorite noodles

1/2 cup Parmesan cheese, grated

parsley (optional)

This is a Cafe favorite that's been on the menu a long time. It's dang good.

JB & Jamie

Shrimp Scampi

Prep Time: 10 min   Cook Time: 15 min   Yields: 4 servings

In a skillet, melt butter.

Add garlic, red pepper flakes, juice from 1 lemon, and a dash of Tony Chachere's Creole Seasoning.

Let mixture cook down and then add wine.

Let wine cook out for 3–5 minutes, being sure not to burn the garlic.

Prepare noodles.

Heat oil in skillet and cook the shrimp.

Strain noodles and toss with Parmesan cheese.

Add wine sauce to noodles.

Plate the pasta and top with shrimp.

Garnish with Parmesan cheese and parsley.

4 tbsp butter

2 tbsp garlic, minced

1 tsp red pepper flakes

1 lemon

Tony Chachere's Creole Seasoning

1/2 cup dry white wine

1 lb of your favorite noodles

olive oil

2 lbs shrimp

1/2 cup Parmesan cheese, grated

parsley (optional)

Super simple but super good for that Cajun fan in the family!

JB & Jamie

JB & Jamie

A Cafe staple! Beautiful presentation! This dish brings out so many colors in the foods and really helps your food pop on the plates as you serve it.

Stir-Fry Pasta

Prep Time: 15 min

Cook Time: 15 min

Yields: 4 servings

Add all veggies to a skillet and pour oil on top.

Season liberally with garlic powder and lemon pepper.

Cover skillet, stirring occasionally letting veggies steam for a while (cooking time varies depending on how you like your veggies cooked).

While veggies steam, prepare noodles.

Strain noodles and toss with Parmesan cheese.

Place veggies on top of cooked noodles and toss in Parmesan cheese.

If you want to add a protein just select your favorite, grill it up, and toss it in with the veggies before you top the pasta!

- 1 small bag broccoli
- 1 squash, sliced
- 1 large portabella mushroom, sliced
- 1 carrot, peeled and sliced
- 1/2 small red onion, sliced
- 10 cherry tomatoes, halved
- 1/4 cup vegetable oil
- garlic powder
- lemon pepper
- 1 lb of your favorite noodles
- 1/2 cup Parmesan cheese, grated
- grilled chicken or shrimp (optional)

The Stir-fry Veggies have become a favorite by so many that we end up making them as a side dish too! Without the pasta they become a perfect side to any of your main courses!

JB & Jamie

DESSERTS

A meal should finish strong with a fantastic dessert. If we go out to eat, you can bet we're going to get desserts, even if we're miserably stuffed. After a salty meal, you need a sweet finisher.

Desserts bring people together. No one goes to someone's house to eat just appetizers or a quick meal and leave, but people will come over just for dessert. Desserts keep the evening of good fellowship from ending too soon. You brew up a pot of coffee, serve dessert, and keep talking.

Of course, Royers Cafe is known for its pies. Not long after Bud started the Cafe, a friend said, "It's not a country cafe without pies." So not only did we start serving pies, but we started mail-order pies.

Our chocolate chip pie became our claim to fame. It was supposed to be the recipe off the back of the Nestlé Toll House Semi-Sweet Morsels package, but we made it wrong, and it ended up being an incredible pie everyone loved. We ended up winning a pie contest. The *Houston Chronicle*, *Texas Monthly*, and other local papers did a story on it, creating a regional and then statewide presence Bud was shooting for. The coverage cultivated what the Cafe became. People wanted to come and see us! Bud used to joke, "We offer a pie-of-the-month plan. Heck, we'll do a pie for life! You write a big check, and we'll send you pies for life."

On Thanksgiving week in 2009, Bill Geist from *CBS Sunday Morning News* picked up on our joke. That day we had 1,200 pie orders and a small catapult to fame. We were featured on *Food Network* and then *The Today Show* in 2016. Matt Lauer actually ate our Texas Trash Pie and made it the number one mail-order pie in the country.

We've simplified these recipes over the years, but the flavor and goodness have only improved. Everything is homemade—no store-bought crusts or canned fruit (except for one recipe that we use canned cherries in to make it super easy for first-time bakers!). Using fresh fruit, a touch of the right spice, and homemade crust elevates simple desserts and makes them worth sharing.

JB & Jamie

We use fresh peaches from Fredericksburg, Texas. They're sweet, juicy, and just phenomenal!

Texas Peach Pie

Prep Time: 30 min

Cook Time: 45–60 min

Yields: 6–8 servings

Preheat oven to 350°F.

Peel and slice peaches.

Cook down peaches and sugar and then drain the excess liquid.

Add a little bit of grapefruit juice to give it a citrus tang.

Roll out pie dough and form into a shell. Set aside leftover pie dough.

Add peaches to the pie shell.

Cut leftover pie dough into 1 1/2 inch strips, and create a lattice top crust by weaving the strips in an over-under pattern (see picture).

Finish top crust by pinching around the edges.

Brush lattice pie crust with melted butter and sprinkle entire pie with cinnamon and sugar.

Bake pie for 45–60 minutes (until crust is lightly browned).

2 1/2 lb fresh peaches

1 1/2 cups sugar

grapefruit juice (optional)

1 10" Royers Pie Crust (p. 243)

cinnamon and sugar

butter, melted

If fresh fruit is out of season, frozen will work. Just know that fresh will always taste better.

JB & Jamie

JB & Jamie

This recipe makes a tad extra,
so we make the rest into cookies. Yummy!

Sweet 'N' Salty Pie

Prep Time: 20 min

Cook Time: 45 min

Yields: 6–8 servings

Instructions	Ingredients
	16 tbsp (2 sticks) butter, softened
Preheat oven to 300°F.	1 1/2 cups white sugar
Beat butter, sugar, eggs, and vanilla until light and fluffy.	2 eggs
	2 tsp vanilla
Combine flour, cocoa, baking soda, and salt.	2 cups flour
Stir into the butter mixture until well blended.	2/3 cup unsweetened cocoa powder (Hershey's)
Mix in the chocolate chips and caramel bits.	3/4 tsp baking soda
	1/2 tsp salt
Roll out pie dough and form into a pie shell.	1 cup chocolate chips
Fill pie shell with mixture and top with sea salt.	1 1/2 cups caramel bits
Bake at 300°F for 45 minutes.	1 10" Royers Pie Crust (p. 243)
	sea salt

This is a perfect combination of salt and sweet coming together. It's so good that it earned itself a name as one of the Top 5 Chocolate Desserts by the *Food Network*!

— JB & Jamie —

JB & Jamie

This was a fun experiment that has now become a fun favorite. Your taste buds are in for a great surprise with a cool tart zing!

Pink Lemonade Pie

Prep Time: 15 min

Cook Time: 0 min

Yields: 6–8 servings

Mix all ingredients together and pour into pie crust.

Freeze 4–6 hours.

Chill until ready to serve.

Garnish with sliced lemon.

1 10" graham cracker crust (p. 243)

8 oz cream cheese (room temperature)

14 oz can sweetened condensed milk

1 can pink lemonade concentrate

8 oz tub Cool Whip

1 lemon, sliced (optional)

When you think of summer, you think of lemonade. On a hot day, this pie is refreshing and tart.

You can serve this one right from the freezer or let it thaw first. Both are amazing!

JB & Jamie

DESSERTS

Texas Trash Pie

 Prep Time: 15 min   **Cook Time:** 45 min   **Yields:** 6–8 servings

Preheat oven to 350°F.

Roll out pie dough and form into a pie shell.

Mix all ingredients together and put in pie crust.

Bake for 45 minutes.

1 cup chocolate chips

1 cup caramel bits

1 cup pretzels, crumbled

1 cup graham crackers, crumbled

1 cup coconut

1 cup pecans

8 tbsp (1 stick) butter, melted

14 oz can sweetened condensed milk

1 10" Royers Pie Crust (p. 243)

Matt Lauer ate this pie on *The Today Show*. It became the number-one mail-order pie of 2016.

JB & Jamie

We just started serving this pie, and of all our pie varieties, this one is hands-down a favorite.

Coconut Cream Pie

 Prep Time: 30 min   **Cook Time: 30 min**   **Yields: 6–8 servings**

Preheat oven to 375°F.

Roll out pie dough and form pie shell.

Bake pie crust for 15–20 minutes until lightly golden brown. Set Aside.

1 10" Royers Pie Crust (p. 243)

Stir cornstarch and salt in a saucepan.

1/2 cup cornstarch

Whisk in whole milk and condensed coconut milk.

1/2 tsp salt

Cook over medium heat, stirring constantly. Bring to a boil and let boil for 1 minute.

1 1/2 cups whole milk

14 oz can condensed coconut milk

In a separate bowl, whisk egg yolks and sugar together.

4 egg yolks, beaten slightly

Add 1/3 of the milk mixture to the egg mixture to temper the eggs.

3/4 cup granulated sugar

Pour the warm egg mixture back into the saucepan and boil for 1 minute. Remove from heat.

2 tsp vanilla

3 tbsp butter

Add vanilla, butter, and 1 cup shredded coconut.

1 1/2 cups finely shredded coconut

Let it cool and then pour into the prepared, cooked pie crust.

8 oz whipped cream (p. 242)

Place in refrigerator to cool and set.

1/8 cup coconut for toasted coconut

Put additional coconut in skillet on stove and toast until light brown.

Finish pie with whipped cream and toasted coconut.

Royers Original Buttermilk Pie

Prep Time: 15 min

Cook Time: 1 hour

Yields: 6–8 servings

Preheat oven to 350°F.

Cream butter and sugar together.

Add eggs and flour to sugar mixture.

Blend in buttermilk, nutmeg, and vanilla.

Roll out pie dough and form into a pie shell.

Pour mixture into pie shell.

Bake 1 hour or until set and knife inserted in center of pie comes out clean.

- 1/2 cup butter, softened
- 3 cups sugar
- 3 eggs
- 1/4 cup flour
- 1 cup buttermilk
- 3/4 tsp nutmeg
- 1 tbsp vanilla
- 1 10" Royers Pie Crust (p. 243)

A staple at the Cafe since 1987 and Jamie's favorite pie!

JB & Jamie

JB & Jamie

A hint of lemon, blueberry filling, and granola topping give you the tart, sweet, and crunch all in one bite.

A Best Seller and a Cafe favorite!

Royers Blueberry with Granola Topping Pie

 Prep Time: 30 min   **Cook Time: 45 min**   **Yields: 6–8 servings**

Preheat oven to 350°F.

Mix flour and water together. Set aside.

In braising pot, bring blueberries, sugar, and lemon juice to a boil.

Add flour mixture and stir until well blended.

Roll out pie dough and form into a pie shell.

Pour into pie shell.

Top with Granola Topping.

Bake pie 45 minutes or until filling is bubbly and topping is golden brown.

Granola Topping

Combine brown sugar, cinnamon, oatmeal, flour, salt, and nutmeg.

Mix thoroughly.

Add butter and mix until equal consistency.

- 3/4 cup flour
- 1 cup water
- 4 1/2 cups blueberries, frozen
- 1 cup sugar
- 1 tbsp lemon juice
- 10" Royers Pie Crust (p. 243)
- granola topping

Granola Topping

- 1 cup brown sugar
- 1/2 tsp cinnamon
- 1 cup oatmeal
- 1/2 cup flour
- 1/4 tsp salt
- 1/4 tsp nutmeg
- 6 tbsp butter, melted

DESSERTS

219

Bob Pastorio's Cherry Pie

Prep Time: 15 min

Cook Time: 40–45min

Yields: 6–8 servings

Preheat oven to 425°F.

Roll out pie dough and form into a shell. Set aside leftover pie dough.

Pour cherry pie filling evenly into unbaked pie crust.

Cut leftover pie dough into 1 1/2 inch strips and create a lattice top crust by weaving the strips in an over-under pattern (see picture).

Finish top crust by pinching around the edges.

Sprinkle with butter, cinnamon, and sugar.

Bake 40–45 minutes or until crust is golden brown.

1 10" Royers Pie Crust (p. 243)

2 21-oz cans cherry pie filling

2 tbsp butter, melted

cinnamon

sugar

If you're new to making pies, start with this one. It's an easy, traditional favorite using canned filling. Finish off with a lattice crust, top with cinnamon and sugar, and boom! Simple and delicious!

— JB & Jamie —

DESSERTS

JB & Jamie

Cooking Tip: Place a cookie sheet under your pie in the oven while it is baking just in case the pie bubbles over!

This one is messy but it is delicious!

Not My Mom's Apple Pie

Prep Time: 30 min   **Cook Time: 50 min**   **Yields: 6–8 servings**

Preheat oven to 350°F.

Peel, core, and cut apples into chunks.

Roll out pie dough and form into a pie shell.

Mound apples in the pie shell.

Combine brown sugar, whipping cream, and flour to make filling.

Pour mixture over apples.

Press crumble topping on apples and filling. Make sure apples are covered.

Bake 50 minutes or until apples are soft and topping is crispy.

CRUMBLE TOPPING

Combine brown sugar, flour, cinnamon, butter, and pecan pieces.

Mix thoroughly.

5–6 Granny Smith apples

1 10" Royers Pie Crust (p. 243)

1 1/3 cups brown sugar

2/3 cup whipping cream

1/4 cup flour

CRUMBLE TOPPING

1 cup brown sugar

3 tbsp flour

2 tsp cinnamon

2 tbsp butter, melted

1/2 cup pecan pieces, finely chopped

JB's dad used his mom's recipe to make apple pie, but she didn't like the way he made it (even though it was her recipe). She said, "That's not my apple pie." Dad said, "Well, we'll call it 'Not My Mom's Apple Pie' and sell it this way." We tweaked the recipe a bit by throwing in some pecans and brown sugar on top and made a fantastic apple pie for the Cafe.

JB & Jamie

Ann's Pecan Pie

Prep Time: 15 min

Cook Time: 50–55 min

Yields: 6–8 servings

Preheat oven to 350°F.

Mix together butter, sugar, corn syrup, salt, and vanilla.

Beat eggs until very light.

Add corn syrup mixture to eggs.

Roll out pie dough and form into a pie shell.

Pour mixture into pie shell.

Arrange pecan halves on top.

Bake 50–55 minutes or until filling is set and knife inserted in center of pie comes out clean.

- 1/3 cup butter, melted
- 1 cup sugar
- 1 cup light Karo corn syrup
- 1 tsp salt
- 1 tbsp vanilla extract
- 4 eggs
- 1 10" Royers Pie Crust (p. 243)
- 1 1/2 cups pecan halves

This is a tribute to the *Houston Chronicle*'s retired food editor, Ann Criswell, who recently passed away. It was one of our top mail-order pies. Since we use a light Karo syrup instead of the traditional dark Karo, it's not too sweet.

JB & Jamie

JB & Jamie

This pie is also known as the Crackberry Pie! It's the Junk Gypsies' fave pie! It's exactly what you'd expect from the name. You take all your leftover fruit and throw it into a pie, like a fruit smash.

Royers Junkberry Pie

Prep Time: 30 min   **Cook Time: 50 min**   **Yields: 6–8 servings**

Preheat oven to 350°F.

Combine sugar, flour, apples, blueberries, raspberries, strawberries, peaches, and blackberries in a sauce pan.

Cook until boiling.

Roll out pie dough and form into pie shell.

Pour mix into pie shell.

Spread topping on fruit filling and sprinkle with sugar.

Bake 50 minutes.

Topping should be firm and golden brown around edges.

Serve pie with a spoonful of Junkberry Topping.

3/4 cups sugar

3/8 cup flour

1 Granny Smith apples, peeled, cored, and sliced

1 cup frozen blueberries

1/2 cup frozen raspberries

1 cup frozen strawberries

1 1/2 cups frozen peaches

1 cup frozen blackberries

1 10" Royers Pie Crusts (p. 243)

sugar for sprinkling

Junkberry Topping (p. 242)

Bud the PieMan says, "This pie is addicting! You will keep coming back for more!". It tends to be a fun favorite for a breakfast snack too!

JB & Jamie

DESSERTS

Big Maw-Maw's Brownies

Prep Time: 20 min   **Cook Time:** 25–30 min   **Yields:** 8 servings

Preheat oven to 350°F.

Mix together butter and cocoa. Set aside.

Mix sugar and flour together. Fold in eggs.

Add the butter and cocoa mixture.

Add vanilla.

Grease and flour a 9" x 9" baking pan and pour mixture into it.

Bake at 350°F for 25–30 minutes.

Garnish with mini chocolate chips.

ICING

Mix together powdered sugar, cocoa, butter, and vanilla.

After brownies are cool, top with icing.

- 8 tbsp (1 stick) butter, softened
- 6 tbsp unsweetened cocoa powder (Hershey's)
- 2 cups sugar
- 3/4 cup flour
- 4 eggs
- 1 tsp vanilla
- mini chocolate chips (optional)

ICING

- 1/2 box powdered sugar
- 3 tbsp unsweetened cocoa powder (Hershey's)
- 4 tbsp butter
- 1 tsp vanilla

Jamie's grandma made these brownies, and they're unlike any you've ever tried. They're fudgy and topped with icing. Growing up, she'd always have a plate on the table ready for us when we visited.

JB & Jamie

DESSERTS

Gluten-Free Peanut Butter Cookies

 Prep Time: 10 min   Cook Time: 10 min   Yields: 8 servings

Preheat oven to 300°F.

Mix all ingredients together well.

Roll into 1" balls.

Flatten rolled cookie balls onto cookie sheet with a fork in a criss-cross pattern.

Sprinkle with sugar.

Bake 10 minutes.

4 cups sugar

4 cups crunchy peanut butter

4 eggs

We cater these at events. You can make the dough ahead of time and freeze it in serving-size balls to cook anytime.

JB & Jamie

JB & Jamie

Jamie always take her cookies out when they don't look quite done. She lets them rest on the cookie sheet for a few minutes before transferring them to a cooling rack.

Barbie's Chocolate Chip Cookies

Prep Time: 20 min   Cook Time: 8–11 min   Yields: 8 servings

Preheat oven to 375°F.

Beat shortening, brown sugar, milk, and vanilla.

Add eggs and beat until fluffy.

Stir in flour, salt, and baking soda. Mix again.

Stir in chocolate chips and pecans.

Spoon cookies (approx. 1 tbsp each) onto cookie sheet.

Bake 8–11 minutes.

1 1/2 cups Crisco shortening

2 1/2 cups light brown sugar

4 tbsp milk

2 tbsp vanilla (Molina Mexican preferred)

2 eggs

3 1/2 cups all purpose flour

2 tsp salt

1 1/2 tsp baking soda

2 bags Ghirardelli milk chocolate chips

1–2 cups pecans, roughly chopped (optional)

With many years of trying out recipes for the tastiest chocolate chip cookies . . . we know this one is our winner! Our girls love them as the perfect ends to an ice cream sandwich!

JB & Jamie

DESSERTS

Granny's Snickerdoodle Cookies

 Prep Time: 15 min   **Cook Time: 8–10 min**   **Yields: 8 servings**

Preheat oven to 400°F.

Cream butter and sugar. Add eggs and beat well.

Sift flour, cream of tartar, and baking soda together.

Combine flour and butter mixture. Blend well.

Roll dough into balls the size of walnuts.

In a bowl, mix together 2 tbsp sugar and 2 tbsp cinnamon.

Roll each cookie dough ball fully around in the cinnamon/sugar mixture.

Place 2" apart on ungreased cookie sheet and bake 8–10 minutes.

Immediately remove from cookie sheet to cool.

16 tbsp (2 sticks) butter, softened

1 1/2 cups sugar

2 eggs

2 3/4 cups flour

2 tsp cream of tartar

1 tsp baking soda

2 tbsp sugar

2 tbsp cinnamon

For a cinnamon fan, these are it. Eat them warm, or freeze them and make a vanilla ice cream sandwich. They're simple and perfect.

— JB & Jamie —

JB & Jamie

This is JB's favorite cookie! His grandma came up with this recipe, and she didn't make them gooey. She made them thin and crispy. When he visited her, she always had a plate of them.

Sugar Cookies

Prep Time: 10 min   Cook Time: 8–10 min   Yields: 8 servings

Preheat oven to 350°F.

Line a cookie sheet with parchment paper (they make parchment sheets now that we always keep on hand for making cookies).

In a bowl (Bowl 1): mix flour, cornstarch, baking soda, and salt. Set aside.

In a seperate bowl (Bowl 2): mix together sugar and butter.

In a seperate bowl (Bowl 3): beat eggs and vanilla with a mixer.

Combine sugar/butter (Bowl 2) mixture with egg mixture (Bowl 3). Mix well.

Start adding the flour mixture (Bowl 1) a little bit at a time to make sure it is all incorporated.

Roll into balls, and place on baking sheet.

Sprinkle with sugar and pop into the oven for 8–10 minutes or until lightly browned!

*parchment paper

2 1/2 cups flour

2 1/2 tsp cornstarch

1 tsp baking soda

1/2 tsp salt

1 1/2 cups sugar

16 tbsp (2 sticks) butter, melted

2 eggs

2 1/2 tsp vanilla extract

sugar for sprinkling

DESSERTS

JB & Jamie

We use our Cafe yeast rolls to make this, and it's become a Cafe favorite. We can't make enough of it. As long as I don't drink the brandy, we can keep making this!

Brandy Pecan Bread Pudding

Prep Time: 30 min   Cook Time: 35–45 min   Yields: 8 servings

Preheat oven to 300°F.

Grease a 9" x 13" pan.

In a bowl, mix together sugar, eggs, milk, and vanilla.

Pour over cubed bread, and let set 10 minutes.

In another bowl, mix and crumble brown sugar, butter, and pecans.

Pour bread mixture into greased pan.

Sprinkle brown sugar mixture over the top.

Bake for 35–45 minutes or until set.

Pour Bread Pudding Sauce over bread pudding.

Bake an additional 10 minutes.

BREAD PUDDING SAUCE

Mix together sugar, butter, egg, and vanilla in a sauce pan.

Cook over medium heat, stirring until sugar is melted.

Add brandy and stir well.

---

1 cup sugar

5 eggs, beaten

2 cups milk

2 tsp vanilla extract

3 cups cubed bread allowed to go stale overnight (we use our yeast rolls)

2 cups light brown sugar, packed

4 tbsp butter, softened

1 cup pecans, chopped

SAUCE

1 cup sugar

8 tbsp (1 stick) butter, melted

1 egg, beaten

2 tsp vanilla

1/4 cup brandy

JB & Jamie

At the Cafe, we serve this in Mason jars, so the presentation is fun, easy, and beautiful. This is pretty fast to whip together and easy way to serve something light and yummy!

Cyndi's Decadent Banana Puddings

Prep Time: 20 min

Cook Time: 0 min

Yields: 4 servings

Combine 2 pudding packages with cold milk and mix with wire whisk for 2 minutes. Set aside to thicken.

Line bottom of a 9" x 13" pan with vanilla wafers (save a few to crush for topping).

Place sliced bananas on top of vanilla wafers.

Combine condensed milk with pudding and fold in Cool Whip.

Pour 1/2 of pudding mixture over wafers and bananas.

Repeat wafer and banana layers.

Pour remaining pudding mixture over last layer of bananas.

Sprinkle top with crushed vanilla wafers.

Refrigerate until ready to serve.

1 3.4 oz package instant French vanilla flavored pudding

1 3.4 oz package instant cheesecake flavored pudding

4 cups cold milk

1 box vanilla wafers

4–5 bananas

14 oz can sweetened condensed milk

16 oz Cool Whip

Variation: Use sugar-free, reduced-fat, or fat-free products.

JB & Jamie

DESSERT EXTRAS

Whipped Cream

Put heavy cream in a mixing bowl and whip on medium for 1 minute.

Add vanilla extract and slowly add powdered sugar.

Whip to desired consistency.

1 cup cold heavy cream

3 tbsp powdered sugar

1/2 tsp vanilla extract

Junkberry Topping

1 cup sour cream

1/4 tsp salt

1 cup flour

1 1/4 cup sugar

Mix sour cream, salt, flour, and sugar together.

Royers Pie Crust

Dissolve salt in milk. Set aside.

Cut shortening into flour, working thoroughly until mixture is crumbly.

Add milk-salt mixture to flour mixture. Work together until liquid is absorbed. If needed, add several tablespoons of flour and continue working dough until it pulls cleanly away from hands.

Divide dough into 3 equal balls.

Freeze in plastic bags until needed.

1/4 tsp salt

1 cup milk

2 cups minus 3 tbsp Crisco shortening (blue label)

5 cups flour

Yields: 3 10" Crusts

Dough rolls out easier when chilled. When using frozen dough: set out 3-4 hours or thaw in refrigerator overnight.

— JB & Jamie —

Graham Cracker Crust

Crush graham crackers in a blender.

Mix together crushed graham crackers, sugar, and butter.

Press into a 10" pie pan.

Bake at 325°F for 10 minutes.

Let cool before filling.

1 1/4 cups graham cracker crumbs

1/4 cup sugar

1/3 cup unsalted, butter, melted

Yields: 1 10" Crust

SAUCES & SEASONINGS

All the blends and sauces in this book are simple to make, but they draw out the intense flavors of our food to push them over the edge. They're all homemade—nothing prepackaged or full of processed junk. And I'll tell you this: they're good.

The seasonings are the foundation for all of our recipes. Because we cook everything on a flat top, we add a lot of pepper and grilling seasoning to meats to give them a crust. As we demonstrate in our Cooking Classes, the meat recipes are cast-iron friendly, so you can cook them in your own home and achieve the same high quality sear.

At the Cafe, we use a lot of the same seasoning for our grilled shrimp, fish, and chicken—often lemon pepper mixes because the taste is delightfully light and refreshing. But if we fry them, we use different flavors and a different seasoning. Lemon pepper doesn't pair well with frying so we use a heavier mix of seasonings.

I can't stress this enough: we always use what we like, and you should too. Think beyond basic salt and pepper. I would tell you there's never too much garlic, but Jamie disagrees. This is where you should be as bold as a chef. Think outside the box, and don't be afraid to experiment with flavors. Just be mindful of what goes well with what you're cooking. You don't want fajitas with mashed potatoes, right? You'll learn from trial and error—and don't let the fear of messing up stop you. Often the most funny family stories start with a cooking experiment that went wrong. If you like a specific seasoning that isn't included in our recipes, try it anyway and see if you like it.

When you find a blend that you just keep raving about (this often happens when you accidentally try mixing a few of your favorite flavors), make sure you write it down and use it again. You will find that more often than not it will become a household standard in your cooking and you have now created your own unique seasoning!

Royers Blue Cheese Dressing

Combine mayonnaise, onion, lemon juice, buttermilk, garlic powder, black pepper, blue cheese crumbles, cottage cheese, cream cheese, and sour cream.

Mix well.

Store in covered container in the refrigerator.

2/3 cup mayonnaise

1/3 cup onion, chopped

1/3 tbsp lemon juice

1/3 cup buttermilk

1/3 tsp garlic powder

pinch of black pepper

2 1/2 tbsp blue cheese crumbles

2 1/2 tbsp small curd cottage cheese

2 1/2 tbsp cream cheese, softened

2 1/2 tbsp sour cream

Royers Creamy Cajun Sauce

Whisk together mayonnaise, Frank's RedHot, horseradish, garlic, and juice of lemon.

Store in covered container in the refrigerator.

3 cups mayonnaise

1 1/3 cups Frank's RedHot

5 tbsp horseradish

7 garlic cloves, grated

1/2 lemon

We put this sauce on our Mike's Fish Tacos (p. 183) and our Tiny Cajun's Fried Green Tomatoes (p. 33).

Another universal sauce! This one pairs well with seafood, somewhat like a remoulade. We've also mixed it with cabbage for a delicious slaw and finishes with a spicy kick.

JB & Jamie

Royers Ranch Dressing

Mix all ingredients in a bowl.

Store in fridge for an hour before serving to let it thicken.

Store in covered container in the refrigerator.

1 cup buttermilk

1 cup sour cream

1 1/2 tbsp apple cider vinegar

1/2 tsp dry mustard

1 tsp garlic, minced

2 tsp dried chives

1/2 tsp dry dill

1 tsp onion, chopped

1 tsp parsley

salt and pepper

We actually started making this for a kids' Cooking Class. The key is to let the dressing sit so it thickens up.

JB & Jamie

Royers Cilantro Ranch Dressing

Chop cilantro in food processor with jalapeños.

Combine mixture with mayonnaise, buttermilk, and ranch dressing mix.

Mix well.

Store in covered container in the refrigerator.

4 oz cilantro

2 small jalapeños

1 cup mayonnaise

1 cup buttermilk

1 oz package dry ranch dressing mix

This is a universal sauce. It can be used as a salad dressing, a topping on a sandwich or taco, and as an amazing dip which helps cool down the spicy bites!

It is a perfect dip for stuffed jalapeños!

JB & Jamie

Royers Honey Mustard Dressing

Mix mayonnaise and mustard until well blended.

Add honey, vinegar, and cayenne. Blend well.

Keep in covered container in the refrigerator.

1 1/3 cup mayonnaise

1/3 cup mustard

1/3 cup honey

1/3 tbsp vinegar

1/3 tsp cayenne pepper

This Royers Honey Mustard Dressing is so good. Everyone at the Cafe always asks for more. You can use it as a dressing, but you can also use it as a dipping sauce or a drizzle to top off a meat.

This takes fried chicken to new heights!

JB & Jamie

Peach 'N' Pepper Glaze

Mix all ingredients together in a pot on the stove and bring to a boil.

8 oz peach preserves

1/2 cup water

handful of pickled jalapeños

1/4 cup honey

Top pork tenderloin (p. 159) with this glaze for a yummy meal, or top cream cheese with this for a charcuterie board.

— JB & Jamie —

Micah's Sauce

Heat olive oil in a large skillet.

Add shrimp, minced garlic, and red pepper.

Cook until the shrimp are half cooked.

Add tomatoes, basil, lemon juice, Seasoned Salt, and Parmesan cheese.

Continue cooking until tomatoes are slightly soft.

Add wine.

Bring to a boil and then simmer until shrimp are done.

1/4 cup olive oil

1/2 pound peeled shrimp with tails

4 tbsp minced garlic

1 tsp crushed red pepper

4 cups diced tomatoes

1/4 of a cup fresh basil, chopped

1/2 lemon, squeezed

2 tsp Seasoned Salt

1 1/2 cups of Parmesan cheese

2 cups Chardonnay

Royers Horseradish Dressing

In a mixing bowl, combine sour cream, horseradish, lemon juice, white pepper, and salt. Stir until well blended.

Store in covered container in the refrigerator.

1 1/2 cups sour cream

2/3 cup horseradish, grated

1/2 tsp lemon juice

pinch of white pepper

1/2 tsp salt

We could eat this stuff on a stone, and it would be good. But since stones will break your teeth, try it on fried oysters or steak.

This creamy sauce is a great dipping sauce for beef tips!

—— JB & Jamie ——

Chimichurri Sauce

Rough-chop parsley and cilantro. Place in food processor and pulse a few times.

Add all remaining ingredients except olive oil.

Turn processor on, and slowly add olive oil.

Process until sauce forms.

1 1/2 cups fresh parsley

1 cup cilantro

1 tsp dried oregano

1 shallot

5 garlic cloves

3 tbsp red wine vinegar

2 tbsp lemon juice

1/2 tsp salt

1/2 tbsp red pepper flakes

3/4 cup olive oil

Use it as a sauce or put it on anything!
Add more red pepper flakes if you like it spicy!

—— JB & Jamie ——

Wren Sauce

Mix all ingredients together.

You will probably want to make a lot of this to use on sandwiches or to dip your fries or chips in.

1/2 cup mayonnaise

3 tbsp ketchup

2 tbsp chopped dill pickles

1-1/2 tsp sugar

1-1/2 tsp white vinegar

Lemon Garlic Basil Sauce

Combine all ingredients and mix in food processor on high. Blend until basil is diced.

2 cups olive oil

1 cups lemon juice

1/4 cup garlic, chopped

1/3 cup basil, chopped

2 tsp salt

2 tsp course ground black pepper

2 tbsp mustard

This sauce goes great on chicken, lamb, pasta, kebobs, and vegetables (especially steamed broccoli) on a hot summer day. We even like it as a salad dressing.

JB & Jamie

Royers Awesome Steak Sauce

Put Royers Dill Butter in large skillet with rosemary, red onion, and mushrooms.

Cook until onions are translucent.

Add red wine and Bud's Marination.

Let wine cook out, constantly stirring for about 2 minutes.

Add heavy whipping cream.

Lower flame to low and let sauce thicken.

Use as a topping for steak filets or as a dip for rolls.

1/4 cup Royers Dill Butter (p. 256)

rosemary

1 red onion, diced

8 oz mushrooms, sliced

1 cup red wine

3/4 cup Bud's Marination (p. 257)

1 cup heavy whipping cream

Make a GREAT STEAK even better! This is the "secret sauce" to one of our most ordered dishes!

The best part about this "secret sauce" is that it is amazing for more than just topping a steak! We enjoy watching patrons at the Cafe soak up every last drop with our rolls.

It has become known as the "Awesome Sauce"!

JB & Jamie

Royers Dill Butter

Crush chicken bouillon cube. Completely dissolve it in hot water by cooking it in the microwave on high for 1 minute.

Combine bouillon mixture with butter, dill flakes, garlic, and onion. Mix well.

Sauce keeps well in the refrigerator and is great on most anything (except ice cream)!

1 cube chicken bouillon

1 tbsp hot water

2 cups butter, softened (not margarine!)

2 tsp dill flakes

1 tsp garlic, minced

1/4 cup onion, diced

We use Royers Dill Butter to cook just about everything in the Cafe. It works great on a flat top or cast iron skillet.

JB & Jamie

Bud's Marination

Mix all ingredients together.

1 cup teriyaki sauce

1 cup soy sauce

1 tbsp Worcestershire sauce

1 tbsp Nature's Seasons seasoning

This marinade goes great on all grilled meats and vegetables. We quickly learned that cooking chicken on a flat top with salt and pepper doesn't make an exciting meal. So we made this savory marinade that packs flavor into the meat and vegetables.

— JB & Jamie —

Mae Dell's Gravy

Melt the butter in a large stockpot. Add milk, seasoning, and parsley.

In a separate bowl, mix together flour and water.

Just as the milk mixture reaches a boil, stir in the flour and water mixture. Cook until desired thickness is reached.

The gravy can be made ahead and stored in the refrigerator. Reheat and thin with additional milk if needed.

4 tbsp butter

4 cups milk

1 1/2 tbsp Bud's Meat Seasoning (p. 258)

1/4 cup parsley flakes

1 1/2 tbsp garlic powder

1 1/2 cups flour

1 1/4 cups of water

Royers Meat Seasoning

Mix all ingredients together.

2 cups salt

1/2 cup ground black pepper

2 tbsp Seasoned Salt

1 tbsp garlic powder

2 tbsp paprika

We use this blend for our dredges, chicken fried steak, chicken tenders, and fried chicken. It's simple and delicious, and packs flavor in the layers of fried foods. Experiment with it and try it on the grill!

Just know that it's really salty, so don't over do it!

JB & Jamie

Royers Grilling Seasoning

Mix all ingredients together.

1 cup garlic powder*

1 cup lemon pepper

1 cup coarse black pepper

*Look for garlic powder that is fine like baby powder. We know it sounds crazy but it makes a difference.

This blend goes on anything. Put it in meat dredges, vegetables, French fries—whatever suits your fancy. It gives steak flavor, it blackens, it does everything!

— JB & Jamie —

Royers Herb Butter Mix

Cut cream cheese into 1" pieces.

Put cream cheese, butter, and Worcestershire sauce in mixer. Beat until uniform.

Add Herb Butter Seasoning and mix well.

8 oz cream cheese

8 tbsp (1 stick) butter

2 tsp of Herb Butter Seasoning (p. 261)

1/2 tsp Worcestershire sauce

People love Royers Herb Butter Mix. We like to put it on baked chicken, rolls, and corn on the cob.

Note: Don't use it for cooking because it will break down and curdle (because it has cream cheese in it).

— JB & Jamie —

Royers Herb Butter Seasoning

Mix all ingredients together.

1/2 lb of garlic powder

1.5 oz dill weed

1 oz dried thyme

1 oz dried basil

1/2 oz dried marjoram

1 oz coarse ground pepper

1 tsp cayenne pepper

Note: Make sure to cover your face when mixing!

JB & Jamie

COOKING TIPS

Cooking with Cast Iron

A cast iron skillet is versatile and great for pushing meals to the next level. Since you can use it on a stovetop and in the oven, it's great for searing steaks, frying chicken, and braising. Since it is porous, it holds all the flavors and reinforces the taste of the food you cook in it. For that same reason—never clean it with soap. Soap will ruin it—and definitely don't put it in the dishwasher. Use chain mail to scrub it clean, and then rinse it with hot water and dry it. Some people put it back on the stove and add a little oil to season it.

If you get a brand-new skillet, throw garlic, onions, and bacon in it and let it cook on low with salt and pepper for a long time in order to get that good seasoning started. With a little love and care, it'll last forever. You can pass it from generation to generation and keep the memories of family alive.

Standing Mixer

Get yourself a standing mixer. It'll make your life a lot easier because it frees up your hands to do other things in the kitchen while whipping up a fantastic batch of mashed potatoes, meringue, bread dough, cake batter—you name it.

Meringue

The key to a good meringue is to get your stainless-steel mixing bowl 100% oil free (make sure it is super clean!) and really cold. Put it in the freezer for a while before you use it.

And know this: if it's humid, you'll have a hard time getting it to whip up and give you those beautiful, stiff peaks. If it's a rainy day or the kitchen's hot and steamy, the meringue is probably going to fall. Be mindful and patient, and know that you're going to make mistakes. Meringues are extremely delicate.

Quality Ingredients

To get good meals, you need good ingredients. The best way to guarantee freshness is to support your local farmer or grow a small garden. Herbs, tomatoes, squash, and many other vegetables aren't hard to grow or maintain, and they can thrive in raised beds or patio planters. If farmers and gardens aren't an option, try buying organic fruits and vegetables from your local grocery store. Spending a few extra dollars can elevate your whole plate.

Get Messy

Be willing to try new things! Most people think they prefer simple romaine lettuce, but try making salads with spring mixes, arugula, radicchio, and all the leafy greens available in your grocery. Each one has its own flavor and can pair well with various dressings, cheeses, fruits, *and other flavors. The more you experiment and try different things, the more your tastes will expand, just as mine did!*

Selecting Good Meats

Always know where your meats come from. The more local and organic the better! Look for good marbling and color. Be willing to spend a few extra dollars on good steaks (look for those Prime or Choice labels), but also understand when it's okay to buy a cheaper cut. If you're using a Crockpot, you can buy a tougher, cheaper cut of meat because the slow cooking process will break it down.

Braising

Braising is a great way to infuse meat with flavor and impress your guests. Season some flour to lightly coat your meat, and then use your cast iron skillet and olive oil to sear it. Once you have a nice sear on all sides, take the meat out, and set it aside. Deglaze the skillet with red wine and broth, add some butter and herbs, maybe some vegetables such as potatoes and carrots, and bring it all to a simmer. Then put your meat back in, cover the skillet with foil, and put it in the oven on low—about 325° F—for a very long time (at least four hours). Slow and low is the key. I guarantee you'll have an incredible piece of meat when it's done.

Garlic

Nothing beats fresh garlic. It's so easy to use with all the different tools available. Pre-minced and powdered garlic are fine in a bind, but fresh garlic is the quintessential ingredient.

Good Knives

You don't need a block of 50 knives. Get yourself three or four quality knives—a paring knife for peeling, a chef's knife for chopping, and a serrated knife for breads. It's worth it to spend $100 on a good knife that is weighted, sharp, and will last forever if you maintain it.

Get a good sharpener, and be sure to sharpen the whole blade, from bottom to tip, before every use.

Rice

The key to good rice is equal parts rice and water - and don't overcook it! Be creative, and try various kinds: brown, wild, basmati, jasmine, and many others. We like to make jasmine and add lime juice, cilantro, cumin, and a little salt. It's great with any meat or Mexican dish.

Steaks

Let your steaks come to room temperature before you throw them on the heat. A cold steak on a hot skillet will come out tough. Get a skillet, add Royers Dill Butter, and cook your steak about two to three minutes per side (don't forget the edges!). Then take it off the heat, and let it rest before you cut into it. It will keep cooking as it rests, and those juices will seal themselves in. Cut it too soon, and you're left with a dry piece of meat.

Plan Ahead Big Dinners

Big dinners don't need to be crazy. Prepare as much as you can ahead of time, even a day or two in advance. Have your vegetables cut so you can throw everything together. Plan ahead for marinades and chill times. Some recipes need "rest" time for an ingredient to come back to room temperature or to thaw before the next step. Planning ahead keeps you from having to stay in the kitchen the entire time. You need fellowship too!

A Pan Can Save the Day

When making something messy in the oven be sure to place a cookie sheet under it. Recipes can bubble over. That isn't a bad thing . . . unless you fill your entire house up with smoke from the burn-off! Placing a cookie sheet under whatever you are cooking will catch any drips or overflows and will help with an easy clean up. You will thank us the next time you turn on your oven!

Keep Side Dishes Warm

Cook side dishes ahead of time, and set them in your oven as low as it will go (about 175°– 200° F). With the sides ready and warm, as soon as your steaks or other meats are done, you can pull everything out, ready to serve warm.

Pies

Using fresh rather than frozen fruit makes all the difference. For a while, we used frozen fruit because it's more convenient. One day we ran out of frozen apples and had to make a pie with fresh apples. It came out so delicious, I said, "What the heck! We've compromised by using frozen!" We always say how good our grandmothers' cooking was—that's because they used fresh ingredients. It is the same with the crust. A good crust is very easy to make. Whip up a big batch, roll it into individual balls, and freeze them for future pies. When you're ready to make dessert, pull one out, let it thaw, roll it, and go.

Making Lists

I used to not be a list-maker, but now I write down every task. Once I know everything that needs to be done to serve a meal, I look through it and prioritize - and make sure I don't forget anything!

Serving Guests for the First Time

As you're putting together a plan to entertain, consider your audience and how many people are coming over. When we aren't sure what our guests like to eat, we make steaks with creamy mashed potatoes and salad. We know we can whip them up fast and delicious!

Seasonings

We try to buy organic fresh and dried herbs and spices. If you can grate it yourself, do it. It's a lot better. And remember to replace seasonings after a year. They don't go bad, but they do lose their flavor.

Advice for New Cooks

Don't be scared of the kitchen. I didn't grow up cooking and eating a lot of different foods, but now I can't imagine doing any other line of work. It's not hard. Read through the recipe and study the directions. You'll learn from your mistakes, and your food will get better and better. Cooking is easy and rewarding. The more you do it and enjoy it, the more it becomes a reflection of who you are — a love language.

Thanks for letting us into your home!

We hope you've enjoyed—and will keep enjoying—these dishes that mean so much to us. Even more than that, we hope that opening this book has enabled you to open the door of your home to friends and family as you create new memories, experiences, and joyful times together—whether it's a party of two, just family, or a big shindig.

We've been working at the Cafe and cooking food for friends for more than three decades, and we can tell you *many* stories from the family and friends who have come through the doors over the years. By reading and working through this cookbook, you're now part of that story and our community at large.

Community—that's the entire reason we do life. We would love for y'all to join us in person at a Cooking Class or a Wine Dinner, or visit us at the Cafe. Follow us on Instagram @royersroundtopcafe, and tag us in your photos of meals made using the recipes in this cookbook.

We can't wait to see what you've got cookin'!

ROYERS ROUND TOP CAFE
105 MAIN STREET
ROUND TOP, TEXAS 78954

(979) 249-3611

WEBSITE:
WWW.ROYERSROUNDTOPCAFE.COM

EMAIL:
HELLO@ROYERSCAFE.COM

FACEBOOK:
@ROYERSCAFE

INSTAGRAM:
@ROYERSROUNDTOPCAFE

TWITTER:
@ROYERSCAFE

ONLINE SHOP:
ROYERSROUNDTOPCAFE.COM/SHOP

DATE NIGHTS

PIES WITH A PURPOSE

COOKING CLASSES

CATERING

EVENT PLANNING

SPECIAL THANKS

We are so grateful to all the wonderful sponsors of this book. This work of love wouldn't have been possible without your help, and we're thankful for each and every one of you.

Kim and Marshall Adkins

Laurel and Jeb Bashaw

Cindy Michael and the Croix Family

Beth, Fort, Betsy, Caroline, Elaine, Daniel, and Abigail Flowers

Lori and John Hasskarl

Jane and Ken Page

Charles and Sherri Schugart

Paige and William Simmons Family

The Suffield Family

Jeffrey Cattorini, MD and Allen Sullivan

Tamara and Andy Taylor

Lisa and John B. Walker Family

Heather and F. Howard Walsh III

Francesca, Cosima, and Valentina

The Wren Girls

As an extra thank you . . .

We thought a great way to end this book and to show a tiny bit more of our appreciation was to share one last recipe—our most popular pie! Over half of all of our pie sales continue to be this amazing pie!

— JB & Jamie —

Bud's Chocolate Chip Pie

Prep Time: 10 min   Cook Time: 60-70 min   Yields: 6-8 servings

Preheat oven to 325°F.

Mix sugar, brown sugar and flour together.

Stir in the eggs and then the butter, combining well.

Fold in nuts and chocolate chips.

Spread in the prepared crust.

Bake at 325° for 60–70 minutes or until a knife inserted in the center comes out clean.

This pie freezes exceptionally well, if it lasts that long!

1 cup sugar

1 cup packed brown sugar

1 cup all-purpose flour

2 large eggs, lightly beaten

8 tbsp (1 stick) unsalted butter, melted

1/2 cup coarsely chopped pecans or walnuts

1/2 cup chocolate chips

1 10" Royers Pie Crust (p. 243)

CPSIA information can be obtained
at www.ICGtesting.com
Printed in the USA
LVHW072025110422
715894LV00001B/1